Statistical Audit

AI Assisted A

Companion Textbook to Au

MW00902032

Published by Auditmetrics
Copyright © 2019 Auditmetrics
www.auditmetrics.com
Boston, Massachusetts

Inquiries about statistical issues:

e.winslow@auditmetrics.com

Inquiries about software issues:

support@auditmetrics.com

To obtain free Small Business Auditmetrics V6 software:

https://auditmetrics.com/register.aspx

Foreword

Over the past few years, AICPA and the Multistate Tax Commission have urged the retirement of the traditional block sample in conducting an audit in favor of the properly drawn random sample. The IRS has demonstrated its commitment to this trend by writing directives for communicating nationwide consistency in statistical sampling knowledge and capabilities.

This is part of a trend of using statistical methods and spreadsheets to enhance the effectiveness of all types of audits including forensic auditing. Appropriate use of sampling techniques contributes to reduced cost, speedy implementation, improved audit results, and makes audits more defensible if challenged.

Computer Assisted Audit Techniques (CAATs) or Computer Aided Audit Tools or Computer Assisted Audit Tools and Techniques (also sometimes referred to as CAATTs) is becoming more popular throughout the accounting profession. These tools assist auditors in their search for irregularities in data files, help internal accounting departments with more detailed analysis and support the forensic accountant with extrapolating large amounts of data for further analysis and fraud detection.

Auditmetrics AI software is a further advancement of CAATs that simplifies and automates the statistical sample design process. With the purchase of this book a small business version of the software will be made available. It has the same functionality as Professional v6.3. THE ONLY DIFFERENCE IS FILE SIZE AND FORENSIC ACCOUNTING LIMITATIONS. Professional v6.3 is available online at the Microsoft Store and is intended for businesses that have the capability and need to assess large data sets. Larger datasets make forensic accounting using Benford formula more practical which is an added feature. With this software regular monitoring becomes practical in a package any small business can afford and manage.

What is evolving is the merging of accounting and statistics into a unified system. But most such systems in the market place tend to be large and expensive mega-systems designed for large corporations. The AI software included with this book is designed with a small footprint that can fit on a lap-top. It is intended to provide maximum auditor flexibility and mobility, ideal for small business and business students who are learning the merging of accounting and statistical theory. It is based on over fifteen years of work by Auditmetrics in setting up statistical audit procedures for the Massachusetts Department of Revenue Audit Division.

It is our view the world does not need just another textbook about statistics and accounting. Many practitioner's guides and statistics made easy texts do help inform but the practitioner also needs a quick and easy path to actual workplace implementation. This book software combination is specifically tailored to help the beginner to go from lesson to real world action in a relatively short period of time.

The only investment on the part of the reader is to go through the "Getting Started" document. The quicker the reader becomes comfortable with data input requirements for Auditmetrics software, the quicker one can start the AI process.

Author Notes

All business can profit from conducting internal statistical audits of their accounts and customers. It is always wise to monitor the life blood of a business in more depth than can be derived from general accounting software reports. There is also a growing availability of new high tech tools to aid business in managing such audits. The AI Assisted software included with this book fully integrates statistical methods into the audit to meet the evolving standards of the AICPA, Multistate Tax Commission and the IRS.

Auditmetrics AI is specifically developed with small business as a priority. It is user friendly such that one can traverse the complexity of the statistical audit using a three step process. Each step entails a series of computer guided analytic checkpoints. An auditor can let the software determine the final statistical sample design but there is ample opportunity for the auditor to fine tune the final design.

Fine tuning also includes Excel templates that summarize audit design and results. Certain areas of the worksheets are protected to avoid overwriting critical formulas that can inadvertently alter audit results. One can unprotect the worksheet to make alterations in line with the reporting preferences of the auditor.

For the user a working knowledge of MS Windows, Excel and Access will help in getting quickly up to speed. It has been our experience that most accountants and individuals that self-administer their business are generally well versed in Excel. Access, on the other hand, is a little less understood. An appendix is included to cover the basics of using MS Access. The internet is replete with "how to" sites, many at no cost. They can also be used to fill-in the knowledge gap.

The book is divided into two main sections:

PART I - A discussion of the theoretical underpinning of the statistical audit. Topics include statistical precision (margin of error), variable versus attribute sampling, stratification, detail stratum, sampling efficiency, Neyman allocation, sample projection methods including controlling for statistical error and possible misstatements. It outlines the statistical audit process in a step by step fashion. Included is the use of an online medical claims case study to expedite the learning process.

PART II - describes the use of Auditmetrics® AI software where one can point and click from initial design to final analysis of the statistical audit. The software automatically generates an Excel spreadsheet of the random sample and also other spreadsheet templates to document audit results. Included are discussions of data inputs derived from Excel, MS Access and QuickBooks® standard reports.

If the book is selected for a business or academic continuing education program, the instructor will be provided slides that have been used by Auditmetrics educators for auditor in-service training.

Changes in Version 6 Software

Version 5 data access architecture was based on a direct read of MS Excel spreadsheets and MS Access relational databases. Though this design is user friendly, over time it proved to be problematic. As we expanded our reach to larger corporations and large data sets, version 5 proved to be untenable.

With large data sets the V5 original architecture turned out to have technical and practical limitations. Excel spreadsheet size limitation is a million records. So as we needed to access accounts with several million records, Excel as a direct data read became untenable. Of course an Access relational database can fill the bill but it proved to have file size performance limitations. The user friendly nature of setting up tables and data relationships does come with considerable operational overhead. For example, sampling an account of 10 million records considerably slows processing performance. The latest version of the software has solve the performance problem. The full new V6 professional version can sample accounts containing multi-millions of transactions under a minute.

Large corporations are not subject to such limitations. They can scale up their servers with more sophisticated and efficient data handling server side software such as Oracle and MS SQL Server. But the primary goal of Statistical Audit–AI is to be a resource for small businesses. That more than likely means operations on a desktop or laptop computer.

I must emphasize that we use the term "AI Assisted". The full definition of AI refers to the simulation of human intelligence in machines that are programmed to think like humans and mimic their actions.

Auditmetrics AI Assistance is not at this level. A simple example may help in explaining what is meant by AI assisted. I once gave a graduate student a spread sheet with the formulas to calculate sample size for a stratified random sample. It was based solely on statistical theory.

He came back to me with a concern what I gave him was faulty. He said "some sample sizes are larger than the population from which they are derived". That can happen when financial data is highly skewed or with aberrant outliers which results in very high standard deviations resulting in such illogical outcomes. Auditmetrics, while performing calculations, also does an assessment of potential outcomes and may make adjustments on the fly or Provide feedback

Version 6 has been reviewed by Microsoft involving several technical checks. Auditmetrics is now a Microsoft Partner

Table of Contents

Part 1 – General Principles

Part II – The Auditmetrics® System

Statistical Audit - AI

Statistical Audit Guide

Part I General Principles

Introduction

The purpose of this book is to provide guidance in the implementation of statistical audit procedures. The following pages outline the statistical methodology employed to ensure conformity to accepted statistical audit standards as published by the American Institute of Certified Public Accountants (AICPA). According to AICPA Statement on Auditing Standards (SAS) No. 39 the essential feature of statistical sampling is:

1. **Sample items should have a known probability of selection, for example, random selection**

2. **Results should be evaluated mathematically, in accordance with probability theory**

If just one of these requirements is met, that does not mean that the audit is statistical. For example, auditors, taxpayers, and others will sometimes state they are using statistical audit methods solely because a random number method is employed to select the sample. They may even enhance sampling efficiency by stratifying the random selection process. However, this is not statistical sampling if no attempt is made to evaluate sample findings mathematically (requirement number 2 above). The general statistical discussion that follows summarizes the statistical procedures specifically designed to conform to SAS No. 39. The fundamental principle of statistical sampling is that, although we do not have the resources to examine all transactions in a taxpayer's book of accounts, we can get a fair and unbiased estimate from a smaller manageable subset or random sample if we follow both principles above.

Attribute vs. Variable Sample

There are two basic types of data sampling techniques, either variable sampling or attribute sampling. When data points are measurements on a quantitative numerical scale, they are variable data e.g. weight, length, and in the statistical audit, dollars. Variable sampling is standard for sales and use tax sampling or sampling in any situation where one wants to measure specific dollar quantities, such as total dollars in error or in compliance with regulations or other standards. Variable sampling is the standard for many states in the audit of sales and use transactions. The Internal Revenue Service (IRS) has established statistical guidelines when projecting revenues and/or expenses from a statistical sample. Variable sampling techniques are mostly mathematical formula driven. The fundamental goal of variable sampling is to answer the question of quantity or "how much?"

Attribute sampling transaction data are classified categorically. For example, data tracking whether accounts receivable items are past due could be categorized as "yes" or "no." Attribute sampling is integral to opinion polling and market research where the pollster seeks the characteristics of targeted subsets of the population. In those environments, the data stratifications are situation dependent. For example a pollster or market researcher may be interested in demographic breakdowns of potential customers such as socioeconomic status and gender. There are multiple variations of attributes but to the accountant they should ultimately relate to that all-important variable, dollars.

Attribute sampling is classification dependent. For example, an accountant may want to examine customer base in terms of sex, age category or other sociodemographic classification. These are attributes that are mutually exclusive, and the purpose of the audit would be to answer the question "how many?" are there in each category. There are several types of attribute questions that may be very useful for internal auditing purposes.

Examples of typical attribute sampling tests are:

- 20 of 100 accounts receivable invoices were past due
- 10 of 40 inventory invoices greater than $1,000 contained a signature
- 19 of 20 fixed assets purchases had a supporting authorization document
- 2 of 11 supplier invoices indicated the early payment discount was not taken
- 13 of 211 journal entries were posted to the wrong account

The results of an attribute sampling test, such as those above, are then compared to a criterion previously established. If the test results are worse than the standard, then the test has failed and accounts should be carefully examined for possible remedies. For example, if the acceptable proportion of past due accounts receivable invoices is 3% and the tested rate is 20%, it may be necessary to impose additional controls, retrain staff, and/or alter invoice management procedures to reduce the number of past due invoices.

There are times when an auditor can exploit the benefits of both methods of sampling. The auditor may be interested in revenue and cost estimates (variables) by different segments (attributes) of the business or class of transaction. As mentioned previously, variable sampling procedures are easier to design and implement because the methodology is largely formula driven. The quantitative nature of dollars also provides more information about each unit of observation and therefore, in statistical terms, a more powerful estimate. An attribute sample is a collection of individual observations based on a common classification. Therefore, each data point is part of a collection of observations, each indistinguishable therefore lacking a certain amount of specificity rendering projections with less statistical power.

The Hybrid Approach and the Learning Experience

In this book, we provide a step by step discussion of a sample methodology that combines the characteristics of both variable and attribute sampling techniques. This combined approach is the methodology many states use as their standard for sales and use tax audits. In those audits, the auditor is interested in "how many" transactions in a tax payer's book are in error, such as having a tax not being paid and owing the state additional payments or having paid a tax in error and deserving a credit. But the auditor is not only interested in "how many" transactions are in error, but also what is the dollar volume owed to the state, or "how much" owed in dollar terms?"

It would be impractical to examine all transactions, but a well-chosen representative subset or random sample can be used to project the total dollar amount. The statistical formulas discussed in this book allow the auditor to minimize the amount of statistical error when performing such projections. The hybrid process is a 2-stage estimation process. First the auditor sets up a variable sampling technique to obtain a representative random sample of an account based on dollar value. Once the dollar based random sample is drawn, the auditor goes through a series of steps to determine the validity of the sample using Auditmetrics AI software.

Because accounts are commonly processed in all businesses electronically through standard software such as QuickBooks® and Peachtree®, various key economic characteristics of the total book of transactions is known, usually through standard computerized reports. It is possible to statistically test whether a sample drawn is a valid statistical subset and not an outlier. For example if sample measures, such as total book value, vary greatly from known book value derived from accounting software, then sample validity criteria can be called into question. If that particular sample is termed a "statistical outlier" then a <u>new sample drawn should be drawn</u>? There are a myriad of variables that can be tested in this manner including revenue, expenses, tax credits etc.

Once the sample validation step has been completed to the auditor's satisfaction, the auditor then examines each transaction in the sample to determine if it is in error or whether it matches established criteria. The auditor is making what is called a dichotomous decision: either a transaction is or is not in error. It is a simple yes/no decision and essentially sets up a 2-category attribute (how many in error vs not?) which can be used to determine an error rate for the transactions sampled. Auditmetrics software and templates can be used to estimate the total dollar volume in error (how much in error?).

An ideal entry point for newcomers to audit procedures is to start with the variable sample. It is more standardized than attribute sampling which requires more sophistication in setting up proper stratification, sample size, and sampling error controls. Starting with a variable sample as a convenient entry point. The auditor can always then break down that sample into various attributes. If there is an interesting finding, then a more sophisticated attribute sample can be developed. At the very least, the variable sample starting point allows a quick look at the potential total dollar volume and economic impact of any attribute issues encountered.

The sampling exercise for sales and use tax audits described in this book starts with a variable sample and then morphs into an attribute sample application. Many states and national firms through the Multistate Tax Commission endorse these procedures for sales and use tax audits. In fact the Multistate Tax Commission offers its own statistical audit education program and augments it with tax policy and interstate cooperation discussions.

Below are examples of hybrid approach to statistical auditing:

What is the error rate of paid medical insurance claims. i.e. Due to plan coverage and eligibility requirements benefits are not valid but were paid.	The auditor wants to know not only how many claims have been improperly paid but also the percentage of dollar volume in error.
The data in the journal. What is the amount of deductions not supported by Non-Taxable Transaction Certificates?	The auditor needs to know percent of and specific dollar amount.
Does sales summary reports match up with credit card company reports?	The auditor wants to know if income statement entries match credit card receipts.
How often are invoices voided without explanation?	Here, the auditor wants to know a specific number of invoice error but also its dollar impact.
Do managers record all supplies pulled from inventory in the inventory log?	determine how many supplies not recorded dollar amount

Does the sales supervisor correctly classify sales by state that subject the business to sale taxes?	dollar amount correctly identifying tax liability
What is the percentage of sales are subject to sales tax due to tax authority relative to total sales?	If the auditor asks the question, "Is the percentage 20% of all transactions", attribute sampling could be used. But here the auditor also may want to know the dollar volume.
What percentage of supplies are pulled from inventory subject to sale promotion deduction each month?	Auditor wants to be able to match sales transaction count and volume with recorded cost of goods sold?
What percentage of expenses have been properly recorded for a federal research tax credit.	The auditor wants to know how many and the dollar amount that qualifies for tax credits

The examples above are concerned with the primary question being, how much (dollar volume)? However dollars do not operate in a vacuum. There are always subsidiary personnel, client and organizational issues that need to be explored. Let's take the example of a medical claims adjudication case. In addition to determining the dollar error rate there should also be an examination of such attributes as does it relate to specific staff and claim types, medical office structure and health plan design characteristics. The auditor starts with an assessment of dollar volume slippage in the system but from that point one has to determine which attributes or categories of transactions should be followed up. The attributes therefore provide the basis for the detective work required to make system corrections.

Verifying Electronic Data

The first step in the statistical audit is to receive transaction information in electronic form from a client or from an internal accounting management information system. Once the auditor receives electronic data to sample, the auditor must verify that the data from a client or from internal accounts is correct and complete by reconciling the electronic data received with business accounting system standard reports. This is accomplished by running totals for selected accounts in the data for a given time period, such as a month or quarter. The auditor then compares these totals with the totals from the accounts selected for audit. While one cannot expect the amounts to match perfectly due to timing issues, manual adjustments to accounts, or other reasons, one can expect the amounts to match reasonably close. It is the auditor's responsibility to determine as to whether the data are correct, complete and appropriate for further audit review.

Defining the Audit Population

The audit population is the total book of account transactions from which the sample is to be drawn. One of the first and most important decision an auditor must make is to determine which transactions should be included in the audit population and which transaction should be excluded. For example, clients or MIS personnel may provide an electronic copy of an entire account file. However many transactions in the file may not have implications for the specific audit.

For example if the audit is for a sales tax audit, not all transaction are subject to sales tax. Examination of transaction not subject to sales tax would be a waste of time for both the auditor who must examine the transaction and the personnel who have to pull the transaction. Therefore, it is up to the auditor to eliminate from the audit population as many irrelevant transactions as possible.

It is important that the auditor understands the account's list of transactions and is able to make an informed decision as to which transactions should be included in the audit population and which can be removed. The potential effect of including accounts with no implications for the purpose of the audit reduces sampling efficiency. The potential effect of excluding accounts that do have specific implications is to reduce the validity of the audit results.

What is Stratification?

Stratification is the process of dividing the population of transaction into segments (strata) based on a certain characteristic. In variable sampling, one would stratify the population based on the dollar amount of the transaction.

Why Stratify?

One would stratify on the dollar amount of the transaction to accomplish the following:

1. Gaining sampling efficiency. A stratified random sample will yield more precise results than an unrestricted random sample of the same size.

2. Offsetting effect of extreme values (skewed distributions). To minimize the effect of large invoices on sample based estimates, it be better for the auditor look at 100% of the invoices in the largest dollar stratum. This stratum is the "Detail stratum.

It is important to stress that the methods used to stratify the population of transactions affect only sampling efficiency, not the validity of the sample results.

How to Stratify the Population

An essential concept is that accounting financial populations are not typically evenly distributed; rather, financial data have a skewed distribution. It is also important to note that the purpose of an audit is to survey and project audit results in an efficient manner. Stratification is the methodology that allows this goal to be achieved by strategically adjusting for population extremes due to skewness and is essential for efficient random sampling.

Stratifying the audit population is accomplished by using the dollar amount of the transaction as the basis of stratification. Strata boundaries are determined by specific transaction dollar values into a collection of mutually exclusive categories. The recommended number of strata is usually 3 to 10 which is also the Auditmetrics AI standard. There are several statistical techniques available for determining the most efficient basis for stratifying a population. The first question is how many strata and what should be the cutoff where 100% of the transactions are reviewed? There are some rules of thumb to reasonably determine the number of strata. However, the first step is to define what is called the detail strata, where 100% of the transactions are reviewed.

Detail Stratum

The first step is the determination of statistical outliers, or in the terminology of stratified sampling of the "detail stratum." This is the strata in which one does not rely on a sample but reviews 100% of the transactions. By eliminating the largest transactions from sampling, we reduce the variability (standard error) of the remaining transactions from which a sample will be drawn. This enhances statistical efficiency. There are rules of thumb to determine what size of transaction should be the cutoff for the detail stratum. For example, one rule of thumb is to select all large transactions that account for 25% to 35% of the total book value of all transactions. The detail stratum isolates those high dollar transactions that have the greatest economic impact.

This rule of thumb is useful in most cases. However, if you have access to and can use statistical software like SPSS, SAS, or STATA, then you can use the guidelines implemented in the Auditmetrics software. The software uses a distribution-based criterion. It starts with examining transaction sizes that range from the 90th percentile to the 99.5^{th} percentile.

The table below shows an audit population with a total of 60,916 records. The second column represents the value of the 90th to 99.5^{th} percentile ranging from $901 for the 90th percentile to $26,145 for the 99.5^{th} percentile. When deciding where one should establish the detail cutoff, a certain amount of judgment is required, and past experience is very helpful. It appears from this exhibit that a reasonable starting point would be somewhere between the 99th to the 99.5^{th} percentile. The number of records would be between 609 and 304. That would be between $11,610 and $26,145 for a reasonable detail cutoff. The final decision was to set $15,000 as the detail cutoff. The Auditmetrics software goes through an iteration process and based on the criteria above suggests a reasonable detail cutoff for the auditor.

Percentile	Value	Cumulative	Strata Size
90th	$901	54,825	6,091
95th	$1,890	57,871	3,045
97th	$3,282	59,089	1,827
99th	$11,610	60,307	609
99.5^{th}	$26,145	60,612	304
Total Records =	60,916		

Auditmetrics provides the auditor with these percentile ranks from which an AI guided detail cutoff can be determined. Auditmetrics will suggest a detail cut-off but there can be room to fine tune..

How Many Strata?

There are several methods to determine the number of strata that would result in the most efficient sample in terms of estimating population parameters. They require a more expert knowledge of statistics than can be covered in this text. However, there are rules of thumb that can be useful in selecting the number of strata. One method is to calculate a value called Coefficient of Variation. The coefficient of variation represents the ratio of the standard deviation to the mean (**SD/Mean**), and it is a useful statistic for comparing the degree of variation from one data set to another, even if the means are drastically different from each other. As data become more diverse from the mean, the more statistical error is inherent in the data set. In the statistical audit world, the coefficient of variation allows one to determine how much volatility (statistical risk) one is assuming in estimating population values from sample statistics.

Each stratum is independently sampled, and efficiency is enhanced because in each stratum is a reduction of diversity around each stratum mean that therefore reduces sampling risk within each stratum. All of the strata collectively enhance efficiency when projecting a total dollar amount as compared to a projection from a simple non-stratified random sample of the audit population. The collective efficiency of stratification is measured by Auditmetrics with a measure called *efficiency factor*.

The table below shows a breakdown of coefficient of variation and suggested number of strata can be helpful.

Coeff. of Var.	# Strata
<1	3
1-2	4
2.1-4	5
4.1-6	6
6.1-8	7
8.1-10	8
10.1-12	9
>12	10

Applying the above rule of thumb to the data in the table below, the coefficient of variation is 5.22, so the number of strata for the sampled transactions would be 6.

	Sample Size	Mean	Std. Dev.
$0	96	$42	$33
$100	95	$168	$70
$275	111	$403	$161
$650	169	$849	$422
$1,400	195	$1,738	$1,013
$2,900	360	$1,013	$11,436
>1500	467	$39,140	$103,613
Total		$350	$1,830
Coefficient of Variation = $1,830/$350=5.22			

The detail and number of strata above were based on rules of thumb as discussed above. If you are conducting an internal audit, these criteria are generally acceptable. But, as a note of caution, there are more precise statistical calculations, as used by the Auditmetrics, to determine both the detail cutoff and the number of strata. If the audit is for an official filing with the IRS or state revenue department, Part II of this text will guide you to the statistically proper mix of detail cutoff and number of strata. With the software one can monitor the effectiveness and cost of different detail and number of strata values.

The next question, after the detail and number of strata have been determined, is what should be strata boundaries?

Strata Boundaries

Of the various methods available to determine strata boundaries, many states have opted to use the cumulative of the square root of the frequency method. This method allows for greater efficiency in the sampling process compared with setting the boundaries using judgment only. Using judgment in setting up stratum boundaries may not be the most efficient. A problem with cumulative of the square root method is that there is no rule of thumb as a quick shortcut. The process is laid out step by step below. If you have a working knowledge of Excel, you can systematically determine strata boundaries step by step as outlined below. However auditmetrics AI software automates this process.

Cumulative of the square root of the frequency method

Exhibit 1 illustrates how strata boundaries are determined using the cumulative of the square root of the frequency method, as published by the New York State Department of Revenue.

Step 1   Evaluate the population and determine if transactions below a certain dollar level should be eliminated from being sampled based on the dollar significance of those transactions. In this example, no transactions under $100 will be reviewed. This is a decision that is made using auditor judgment and has no statistical significance.

Step 2   Evaluate the population and determine what the high dollar cutoff will be for detailed review. In this example, all items $10,000 and over will be reviewed in detail.

15

Step 3 Stratify the remaining transactions within the population of items to be sampled ($100 to $9,999.99) using a set ($500). We use $500 for the current example to limit the number of strata that need to be displayed. In actuality, $100 intervals are used by New York State auditors, and $50 intervals are used by the Auditmetrics software.

Step 4 Determine the frequency f(y) for each dollar range. This is nothing more than the number of transactions within each dollar range.

Step 5 Calculate the square root of the frequency for the first sampled range ($100 to $499.99), which is 146.5. Now calculate the square root for the next sampled range ($500 to $999.99), which is 94.1. Because we are accumulating this column, each result gets added to the number before it. The cumulative of the first 2 strata is 146.5 + 94.1, which equals 240.6. Continue this process for each of the sampled strata.

Step 6 Once the cumulative of the square root of the frequency for the final sampled strata ($9,500 to $9,999.99 in this case) is calculated, the strata can be determined. For the final result, 770.1 is divided by the number of sampled strata desired (6 in this case, but can vary between 3 and 9 sampled strata). This result is the test interval of 128.4.

Step 7 The first strata boundary is determined by comparing the test interval of 128.4 against the calculated cumulative of the square root of the frequency for each dollar range and selecting the range that is closest to this test interval amount. In this exhibit, 128.4 is closest to 146.5 for the first sampled dollar range ($100 to $499.99). The second strata range is determined by calculating 2 × 128.4 and finding the closest range. The second strata range will encompass $500 to $999.99 because 240.6 is the closest interval to 256.8. The third strata range is determined by calculating 3 × 128.4 and finding the closest range. The third strata range will encompass $1,000 to $2,499.99 because 401 is the closest interval to 385.2. This process will continue until all 6 sampled strata ranges are determined.

16

Exhibit—1 Cumulative of the Square Root of the Frequency Method

Dollar ranges $500 intervals	Freq. f(y)	Cumulative square root of frequency,	Strata	Strata boundary
0 - 99.99	20,090			*Eliminated*
100 - 499.99	21,472	*146.5*	*1*	*$100 -$ 499.99*
500 - 999.99	8,850	*240.6*	*2*	*$500 -$ 999.99*
1,000 -1,499.99	4,149	305.0		
1,500–1,999.99	2,637	356.4	*3*	*$1,000- $2,499.99*
2,000– 2,499.99	1,990	*401.0*		
2,500– 2,999.99	1,620	441.2		
3,000 3,499.99	1,815	483.8	*4*	*$2,500–$ 3,999.99*
3,500– 3,999.99	1,056	*516.3*		
4,000– 4,499.99	879	546.0		
4,500– 4,999.99	627	571.0		
5,000– 5,499.99	598	595.5	*5*	*$4,000–$ 6,499.99*
5,500– 5,999.99	520	618.3		
6,000– 6,499.99	425	*638.9*		
6,500– 6,999.99	471	660.6		
7,000– 7,499.99	458	682.0		
7,500 - 7,999.99	429	702.7		
8,000–8,499.99	358	721.6	*6*	*$6,500–$ 9,999.99*
8,500–8,999.99	241	737.2		
9,000– 9,499.99	275	753.7		
9,500– 9,999.99	269	*770.1*		
≥10,000	234		*7*	*Detail*

The population profile below in Exhibit 2 summarizes the results from using the cumulative of the square root of the frequency method to determine the strata boundaries.

Exhibit 2—Population Stratification

Strata	Strata boundary	No. of items	Population dollars	Standard
1	$0 - $99.99 (not reviewed)	20,090	738,807	
2	$100-$499.99	21,472	$5,432,668	$109.89
3	$500-$999.99	8,850	$6,368,355	$144.67
4	$1,000- $2,499.99	8,776	$14,041,520	$431.59
5	$2,500- $3,999.99	4,491	$14,103,433	$411.27
6	$4,000- $6,499.99	3,049	$15,469,958	$715.53
7	$6,500- $9,999.99	2,501	$20,025,062	$1,010.2
8	≥$10,000	234	$6,319,170	-

Neyman Allocation

Exhibit 2 shows that 6 strata boundaries (strata ranges 2-7) will be used in selecting a random sample. Strata 8 is not to be sampled but reviewed at 100%. The next issue is to determine what should be the size of the sample in each stratum? Statistical formulas exist to determine optimum sample size that have to meet specific objectives such as precision and confidence levels. The expected amount of statistical error is a key piece of the formula used to calculate optimum sample size. The specific measure of variability that indicates the amount of statistical error in the random sampling process is standard deviation. This section discusses the appropriate formula to calculate an optimal sample size. Once a total sample size is calculated, the next issue is to determine how should that total be distributed among the various strata. Auditmetrics combines both calculations in one formula, simultaneously determine the total size of the sample and allocate the sample among the various strata.

There is a method of sample allocation among the strata that provides the best statistical efficiency. That case of optimal sample strata allocation is called **Neyman Allocation**. Exhibit 3 outlines this allocation method. In the example, we use a sample size **185** to be allocated among 3 strata. The methodology takes into account both transaction count and inherent variability/error (standard deviation) for each stratum.

1. For each sampled strata, calculate the product of the number of items in the strata (N) and the standard deviation for that strata (σ).
2. Sum these products $\Sigma (N \times \sigma)$ for the 3 strata.
3. Calculate what percentage (sample allocation percentage) the product is of the sum for each individual stratum.
4. Multiply the computed percentage by the total sample size for the n sampled strata, 185 in this case.
5. This result is the number of items to be sampled for each of the strata (strata sample).

Exhibit 3 Example of Neyman Allocation of Sampled Items

	N - Freq.	(σ)	(σ × N)	Alloc.	n
$0-200	2,342	39.93	93,516	41%	77 *
$201-400	151	305.56	46,140	21%	38
$401-2,000	184	461.88	84,986	38%	70
>$2,000 (detail)	70				
			224,642	100%	**185**

* = 41% x 185

Exhibit 3 specifically outlines the Neyman allocation process. When actually calculating a proper sample size, sample size and Neyman allocation are calculated jointly using the formula described in the next section.

Strata Sample Size Calculation

The final step is to actually calculate the sample size for each stratum omitting the detail stratum in which all items are assessed. This technique involves the Neyman allocation previously discussed and optimal size determination that takes into account our standards for confidence and precision. That is, the calculated sample size of each stratum is weighted in part by the standard deviation of that stratum. The formula is:

$$n_i = (N_iSD_i)(\Sigma N_iSD_i)/(A/U_R)^2 + \Sigma N_iSD_i^2$$

Where:

n_i = sample size per stratum i

N_i = population size of stratum i

SD_i = standard deviation of stratum i

A = acceptable precision

U_R = reliability factor

No matter which method is used in determining sample size, it is important to emphasize that sample size is based on assumptions derived from statistical theory, particularly the expected precision, statistical confidence level, and assumptions about the distribution of the transactions in the sampling population. Below are the statistical criteria of strata sample size calculation used by the Commonwealth of Massachusetts Department of Revenue Audit Devision.

1. Confidence level- 95% confidence level

2. Required precision: 3% precision (margin of error)

3. Minimum sample size (30) per stratum defined by the Central Limit theorem

Confidence level

The confidence level is an index of certainty. Generally expressed as a percentage or dollar range, confidence level refers to the probability that a true audit population dollar value will fall within a specified range. True population value is the dollar value that can be determined by 100% examination of the account. For example if an audit

22

population has an average of $100, and the auditor states that a 95% confidence interval (CI) around that audit population's actual average is ± $5 or between $95 and $105. This would indicate that 95 random sample estimates out of 100 would be in that range and contain the true value of $100. That would also mean 5% of the sample estimates would be outside of that range.

Precision (margin of error)

Precision is the size of the range one sets within which the true population value would fall. Precision is a value one sets as a precondition in calculating sample size. For example, suppose we have a total book of accounts with a mean value of $100. Suppose the goal is to have a sample estimate within 3% (precision) of the true population mean, the total precision range would be $6 ($97-$103). A precision of 3% would require a larger sample size than a precision of 5% or 10%. Both CI and precision are inputs needed to determine sample size.

A CI of 95% is the generally accepted standard that Auditmetrics uses in calculating sample size. Precision, on the other hand, is what the auditor deems appropriate. A 3% precision is generally considered the gold standard. Its limitation is the narrower the precision range the larger the sample size, but the larger the sample the greater the audit cost.

Precision and confidence levels are generally used together in describing a sample design. A more precise way of expressing this relationship between 3% precision and 95% confidence is by stating that one is 95% confident that sample results would be within a $3 or 3% of the true population value. By the way, in political polling precision is generally referred to as *margin of error.*

Minimum sample size

It is recommended that the minimum sample size in a stratum be 30. In cases where the stratum calculation is <30 transactions, one should increase that stratum's sample size to 30. A sample of 30 is usually considered the smallest sample size where the normal or bell shaped curve can be safely used. It is the normal curve that is used to establish confidence levels. The normal curve is the mathematical foundation of the behavior of random samples upon which confidence intervals are based.

One important observation to note from statistical theory is that there is not direct relationship between the audit population total number of transactions and sample size. This is because the amount of variation or standard deviation of the dollar value has a greater impact on sample size than simply the number of transactions in the audit population. A population of a million records with a large spread of dollar values is going to require a larger sample than a population of a size of 10 million records with a very low dollar spread. Standard deviation measures how compact or diffuse are a book's dollar values. The more diffuse the greater amount of statistical sampling error which in turn requires larger samples.

To accomplish optimum allocation , one should make each strata sample size proportional to both the number of transactions in each stratum and the standard deviation of that stratum, or the Neyman allocation, which was described previously.

In Exhibit 4, exhibit rows 1 to 5 summarize from a statistical perspective all the relevant factors relating to the current sample under review. The Z score of 1.96 indicates that the confidence interval is set at 95%. In row 5, the precision is listed. This value is the total range within which the population value would fall at a given confidence level. The precision, or margin of error, is 3%.

In rows 6 to 9, the strata breakdown for the audit population is listed. Included are the mean, standard deviation, total frequency, and sample size for each stratum. The final stratum, row 9, is the detail stratum. In this example spreadsheet, a total of 255 records are needed to perform the statistically appropriate audit. The audit population is then broken down into 3 sampling strata and the detail strata (>$2,000) where 100% of the records are reviewed. The sample size column lists the number of sampled records required in each stratum (35, 54, 96, and 70).

In rows 10 to 13, totals of the various strata are summarized. The item in row 13 is the efficiency factor. It is beyond scope of this book to fully detail the calculation of the efficiency factor, but it represents an estimate of improvement in statistical efficiency. The efficiency factor indicates the increase in statistical estimation efficiency (84%) due to stratification and elimination of detail stratum transactions from random sampling as compared to a simple random sample that is not stratified and includes the detail stratum. The efficiency factor is a measure of the reduction of statistical error in estimating audit populations values. It is accomplished by stratifying the transactions to be sampled and eliminating large transactions (detail) from the statistical estimation process.

Exhibit 4—Sample Size Determination for Each Stratum

1. 95% confidence Z:	1.96
2. Sample size calculation:	1.85
3. Detail line size (100% of strata):	70
4. Total selected records for audit:	255
5. Precision (error margin):	3%

	N	Mean	Std. Dev.	Total	n
6. $0-$74.99	1,944	$35.12	$15.42	$68,273	72
7. $75-$424.99	556	$170.82	$83.08	$94,976	83
8. $425-$2,000	177	$869.26	$462.52	$153,859	30
9. >$2,000	70	$3,919.18	$2,897.69	$274,343	70
	====	=====	=====	=====	=====
10. Population (excluding outliers)	2,677	$118	$125.24	$317,104	185
11. Detail	70	$3,919	$2,898	$274,342	70
12. Total Population	2,747	$215	$792	$591,446	255
13. Efficiency Factor	84%				

Managing Large Data Sets

Excel has built in functions for many statistical procedures and is a very valuable tool in conducting the statistical audit. However, Excel may be cumbersome to manipulate large data sets. For example the following is an actual book of transactions:

Total Account summary

# Transactions	Mean	Std. Dev.
217,455	$ 10.60	$ 14.52

A book has 217,455 transactions from which we want to draw a random sample. Can we lighten our workload? Is it possible to cut down the total book from which we can draw an audit sample while at the same time maintaining the integrity of the full book? We have done much research in this area including power simulations of random samples as a percentage of total population size. We have found if you take a random sample that is at a minimum 10% the total population, then that subset will fairly mirror the full population. As an exercise let's take a 15% random sample of the population above and see how that subset compares to the whole. Why 15%, just to add a buffer, the higher the percentage the better:

15% Subset Summary

# Transactions	Mean	Std. Dev.
32,618	$10.55	$14.44

As can be seen we now have a subset of transactions that have an average and standard deviation very close to the original total population book. What do we know at this point? We have a subset that has an almost identical standard deviation that drives sample size calculations but a much smaller set of data to work with.

We now have the ingredients for a two-step process:

1. Cut down the original data set to a more manageable number.

2. Draw your sample from the subset.

Let's now conduct an experiment. We will use standard statistical

	Total Book			Sample (15%)	
Strata	Mean	Sample Size		Mean	Sample size
0 -$9.99	$2.68	113		$2.68	112
$10-$24.99	$23.73	38		$23.10	38
$25-$49.99	$29.40	61		$29.76	58
$50-$74.99	$72.34	34		$72.25	34
$75-$160	$90.41	36		$88.71	36
	Sample Size:	282		Sample Size:	278

software, in this case Stata v14, to conduct the experiment. First draw a sample from the total book of 217,455 transactions for an audit. Then a sample from a 15% subset of data of 32,618 transactions and see how they compare. In doing this experiment we will draw a stratified random sample from both sets of data. Below is a comparison of the sample from the total population and a sample from the subset of data.

As can be seen the two samples are very close. It can be demonstrated that both samples provide an almost identical statistical projection. Using what is called the **"Ratio Estimate Method"** of projection, both samples are within a precision of 3% of the total book.

When using the small business version of the Auditmetrics software there is a file size limitation of 100.000 transactions per account to be sampled. When confronted with a dataset that exceeds that limitation then this a good way to reduce the audit population and not lose sampling accuracy. Depending on total number of transactions, you can raise the percentage used for the subset. The professional version of the software does not have a file size limitation and has been tested sampling millions of transactions. It also contains the ability to conduct forensic accounting using Benford's formula.

It should be noted that all calculation results generated by Auditmetrics have been validated by using nationally recognized and accepted statistical software. The software used for these tests was Stata® and SPSS® (Statistical Package for Social Sciences).

Statistical Audit Estimation

To calculate the true value of cost and revenue from a set of transactions, one would have to examine all of the transactions in that book. In practical terms, that is not feasible, especially when an audit population can contain hundreds of thousands or millions of transactions. If an auditor were to collect 1,000 or more random samples and calculate a projection for each and happens to know the true population value, that auditor would observe that half of the sample projections would be above the true population value and half would be below the true population value. Collectively, all the sample estimates would tend to converge onto the true book value in the pattern of the bell-shaped curve, also called the normal distribution. This is inherent in the mathematical behavior of random samples. If a random sample is properly drawn then its behavior is predictable within certain boundaries. Due to the bell shaped curve the auditor would also observe that some sample projections would be beyond the upper or lower 95% confidence limits. Those extreme values would be considered relatively rare i.e. occurring less than 5%.

Sales Tax Audit and Risk

Suppose a state revenue department has set a standard that an acceptable account error rate should be under or equal 3% . If met then only dollars owed the state would be required. If not met (>3%) other additional sanctions may be imposed.

Type I Misstatement - The sample supports the conclusion that the recorded sales tax error rate is ≤ 3% when the audit population or total book sales tax error rate is actually >3%.

Type II Misstatement - The sample supports the conclusion that the recorded sales tax error the value of > 3% but the audit population or total book actually rate is actually ≤ 3%.

		Actual Total Book Error Rate	
		Tax Error <3%	Tax Error ≥ 3%
Error Rate Derived from Sample	Sample says 3% Standard Met	Correct Decision	Incorrect Type II Misstatement
	Sample says 3% Standard Not Met	Incorrect Type I Misstatement	Correct Decision

Controlling Misstatements

Type I Misstatement: Auditmetrics automatically controls the probability of this misstatement at 5%. When calculating sample size using 95% confidence level the Type I misstatement is set at 5%.

Type II Misstatement: Controlling this risk is more complicated than controlling type I misstatement. It usually involves selecting an appropriate sample size to detect a difference of a specified magnitude (precision). If there is a concern when reviewing efficiency factor then the best protection is to select the lowest precision (3%) that results in the largest sample size.

Power and Type II Misstatement: This is often thought of in the context of the **statistical power** to detect a difference of a certain magnitude. The larger the sample size the greater the statistical power which is 1- type II misstatement. A statistical power of 80% is 1-(type II misstatement). The type II misstatement is 20%

Part II – The Auditmetrics® System

Streamlining the Process for Sales Tax Audits

What has been discussed so far is a model of the statistical audit that many states use and the Multistate Tax Commission and AICPA recommend. Also included in this section is a case study of determining the error rate among paid medical claims that follows the same model.

Essential Statistical feature of that model is:

Steps in the Process	Distribution	Data	Data Type
1 .Audit population dollars to be sampled	Unknown, usually skewed	Known from MIS standard reports	Variable
1.Variable sample of Populations based on Dollars	Sample estimates follow normal (bell shaped} curve	Sample Estimated compared to known from MIS	Variable
3.From variable auditor determines dollars in error or not	Dollars based on auditor attribute classification	Unknown, total amount in error est. from sample	Attribute/ Variable
4.Calculate proportion of dollars in error	Binomial statistical properties	Estimate population error rate from sample	Attribute/ Variable

Many steps in the above process are semi-automated by Auditmetrics.

This statistical audit model has a broad range of applications. What we cover is a two-step process starting with validating a variable sample (steps 1 & 2) and then transforming the selected transactions into an attribute of interest, (3 & 4), in this instance a dichotomous attribute of in-error or not in-error transactions . Not all audits are interested in errors. For example an auditor may simply want to determine from a book of expenses those that qualify for an IRS research tax credit so to properly prepare tax documentation.. In that instance, a tax credit rate for the book would be used to determine total tax credits. The IRS has recently allowed an expanded use of statistical sampling, as long as the auditor follows IRS directives.

The Auditmetrics software was designed to make it easy for CPAs and internal auditors to design and select a sample to complete the audit. This is true for whatever type of audit is contemplated. The combining of statistics and accounting has been accelerating because of the growth of information technology. What was once considered exotic has become common-place. Microsoft Excel is a classic example. At first it was an aid in summing and totaling budgets but now, in its latest version, it has a complete array of built-in statistical functions that in many instances replace the need for separate statistical software.

The purpose of Auditmetrics is to help accountants advance their skills in combining statistics and accounting. It was developed for the Massachusetts Department of Revenue Audit Division because of a mandate to get statistical audits implemented as quickly as possible. Software as close to point and click as possible was needed. Getting bogged down in complex statistical discussions and manipulations would interfere with field auditors retiring their traditional block sample in favor of the more effective statistical sample. The goal was to complete the turnaround from statistical audit design to sample selection in a relatively short period of time. The end product of this effort was the Auditmetrics described in the following sections.

Auditmetrics Overview

This section describes the system that streamlines the design and implementation of the statistical audit sampling process. A cutdown version is available on the internet for a following case-study exercise. Use the web based cutdown version to test the impact of changing different inputs to the model.

The following screen image details the Windows software's working parts. The text boxes on the left designate input criteria and the two on the right will contain sample design outputs.

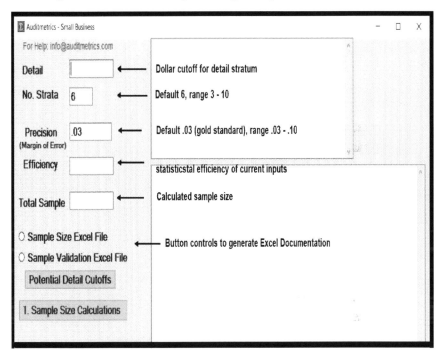

Step 1: Set up data that meets Auditmetrics criteria.

A. **Auditmetrics requires four variables, if not present an error message will be displayed:**

1. **Amount** – The dollar transaction of interest in the analysis.

2. **Absamt** – Absolute value of each transaction. This variable **must** be sorted in ascending order. This is to handle credits.

3. **Transaction_ID** – an identifier for each transaction of the account, in most cases it is a record count.

4. **DataSet** – A name to identify this dataset, valuable for internal controls e. g. date and other account info.

5. **Primary Key- Optional** – If a dataset is from a relational database with a primary key that links with various data tables, it is prudent to include this variable in the audit population to be sampled.

> **Variables 1 to 4 must be in the data file and spelled exactly as above. Any other variables are those relevant for the specific audit to be conducted.**

For the required variables, letter case and order do not matter and absamt **must** be sorted in ascending order. If a dataset is from a relational database with a **primary key** that links various data tables it is prudent to include it in the total book to be sampled. In terms of statistics, total book is the "audit population" from which a sample is to be derived.

Transaction_ID has value when the data set is the merging of several data sources. For example, if you have two data sets of 1000 each and use MS Access to merge them into one file then Transaction_ID 1 to 1000 is from the first dataset and 1001 to 2000 from the second dataset. Transaction_ID also has value when filing with the IRS. For more details review *Appendix III – Random Sampling and IRS Directives* in the book.

A. Data Sources

From the book of transactions to be sampled the simplest data set is to start with an Excel file. The first row of the spreadsheet must contain the required data elements as indicated above. The column named amount is the transaction in which we are interested. Auditmetrics requires only four variables. Any other variables are relevant for the needs of a particular audit but not necessarily required by Auditmetrics. After the first row of the spread sheet all the following rows must be the individual data elements. This is called a rectangular dataset

For most accountants an Excel spreadsheet is an easy starting point. Most good accounting software packages have features to generate data in the form of a spreadsheet. Some accounting systems such as QuickBooks have more proprietary control of their data but it does have standard reports that can be printed or saved as a spreadsheet. Formatted reports are not rectangular data sets but there are methods to convert such reports into a rectangular dataset. This will be discussed in the section on how to convert QuickBooks® standard reports into a rectangular dataset.

Auditmetrics requires a tab delimited text file for data input. It is a simple matter to save the Excel file as a tab delimited text file which is universally accepted by a multitude of products including all major database and statistical software. Conversion from Excel to tab delimited text file is accomplished by using **"save as"** in Excel and select **"tab delimited text"** for file output. You are now ready to get started in designing your audit statistical sample.

36

Excel is a universally accepted software by the accounting profession. However spreadsheets are excellent file management tools but a more versatile data tool included in Microsoft Word is Access Database. Microsoft Access is a versatile relational database system. A relational database (RDB) is a collective set of multiple data sets organized by tables. RDBs establish a well-defined relationship between database tables. Tables communicate and share information, which facilitates data search ability, organization and reporting. Most auditors would benefit greatly by becoming comfortable with using a versatile data base management system. All Excel files can be directly read into Access. Appendix II provides a discussion on how to use Access in creating an Auditmetrics readable tab delimited data file.

Auditmetrics can handle all Excel currency formats including parenthesis for negative numbers. The only exception is negative numbers in red type only, it will not transfer as negative. When sharing data between several software products it is best in Excel to use General format for amount and absamt. Auditmetrics has a powerful parser to handle input data. A problem may arise when sharing data with other software. Each may have its own quirks. The best policy, while in Excel, would be to always format amount and absamt as General rather than currency or accounting format. Auditmetrics can handle most formats but it is best to keep things simple.

If You are using an MS Access Database to generate the tab delimited input file, the data format should be "Number" and Precision "Double".

B. Data Flow from Inputs to Random Sample

It is helpful to examine the input text file before conducting an audit. One can use Microsoft Windows NotePad text editor which can be found in the "Accessories" section of Windows. A more robust editor that can also sort text files is of great value especially when dealing with large datasets. One such product is IDM UltraEdit®. It also has a nice feature of making unprintable tabs visible. In many cases we may have to derive data from a multitude of accounting systems. The value of using tab delimited text files as inputs is that they are universally accepted format for input and output by all major database and statistical software. Some accounting systems like QuickBooks do maintain proprietary data structures. There are options we will discuss later.

In the diagram below on the left are some major data sources that have mechanisms to generate text tab delimited files. In this book we cover the first three. The output random sample files generated by auditmetrics is both a tab delimited text file and a comma separated variable (.csv) text file with the name "sample.txt" or "sample.csv". *The advantage of the .csv file format is it can be directly read in by Excel and immediately saved as an Excel workbook*

Auditmetrics Data Flow

Input Source	Input Data File	Output Sample
Excel		
MS Access		
QuickBooks	=> .txt TAB Delimited =>	.CSV text file*
Oracle		**.txt TAB Delimited**
MS SQL		
SPSS		
SAS		
STATA		

* Can be directly read in by Excel and saved as an Excel file

Step 2 Let's Get Started with Designing a Sample.

As a preliminary examination of the dynamics of the statistical audit process a simplified version of the auditmetrics system is available on the internet. The intention is to help you examine the interplay of the critical inputs in the design of a random sample.

A. Medical Claims Audit Case Study

Background

For several years Auditmetrics has been involved in the design and analysis of health-care plans. Its initial work was with Taft-Hartley labor/management health and welfare funds designing vision, dental and pharmacy benefits. Initially Auditmetrics software was used to analyze the actuarial experience of submitted health insurance claims.

It was later used to do statistical analysis for the Massachusetts Rate Setting Commission which later morphed into the Division of Healthcare Finance and Policy. Auditmetrics was then used to analyze medical claims from Medicaid and all of the state's major health insurers including HMOs and commercial carriers. Teams of auditors and statisticians then used the analysis to establish reimbursement policies for both private insurance and the Medicaid program.

Around the same time the IRS published directives in setting statistical audit standards, and the Federal government also set standards for auditing Medicare claims. When congress passed the Medicare Prescription Drug, Improvement, and Modernization Act it also set up the Recovery Audit Contractor, or RAC, program to identify and recover improper Medicare payments paid to healthcare providers under fee-for-service Medicare plans. Before this act statistical audits of health claims were largely a combination of national and regional standards. Now there is evolving national standards emanating from the nation's largest health insurer, Medicare.

The two primary ways through which RACs identify claim error are "automated review" and "complex review." Automated review occurs when an RAC makes a claim determination without a human review of the medical record. RAC's use proprietary software designed to detect certain types of errors. For complex reviews which no written Medicare policy/articles/coding exists, a review of the medical record is involved. In those reviews, the RAC must use appropriate medical literature and accepted statistical standards. The RAC's medical director must be involved in actively examining the evidence used in making individual claims determinations.

A separate subset of Auditmetrics performs what Medicare defines as an automated review. It is an automated process to identify medical claims with errors such as:

- Incorrect submitted reimbursement amounts
- Prior authorization procedures not properly documented.
- Improper coordination of benefits of separate member and spouse plans
- Non-covered services (including services not reasonably necessary)
- Incorrectly coded services
- Duplicate services
- Paid claims with member eligibility errors

Case Study Web Site

The internet Auditmetrics study version to conduct this case study is available at the following website:

http://www.healthe-link.com/audit/eaudit.aspx

Link to the website. Start with "Potential Detail" to determine a reasonable cutoff and from there start with default number of strata and precision then vary them to determine impact on sample size.

The internet version has the basic statistical functionality of the Windows version. The desktop version uses artificial intelligence (AI) Assistance to design, generate and document a statistical sample. The internet version uses a standard test dataset so that one can test different inputs impact on sample design.

From this case study one could test different input options for detail cutoff, number of strata and precision (margin of error) to assess their impact on sample size. Once a final design is accepted the results are displayed in screens #1 and #2 on the right. The screens are tab delimited. That means columns may not quite align on the screen but if you copy and paste them onto an Excel spreadsheet, the columns will line up correctly. A transfer to Excel allows you to manipulate and analyze what is displayed on the screen. The Windows version generates Excel files directly that will be used for sample documentation and analysis.

Detail Cutoff

The dataset available on the web site is a simulation of actual claims data with a known error rate of 10.2%. The first step in the design phase is to determine the detail cutoff. Click on the button as indicated below:

41

Percentile:	Cutoff	Cum, Count	Detail Size
90th	325	8432	1048
95th	484	9956	524
97th	**744**	**10166**	**314**
99th	**1896**	**10376**	**104**
99.5th	2500	10429	52
Total Frequency-->		**10480**	

By clicking the on the "Potential Detail" button, the data set is broken down into percentile ranks. As the directions on the screen indicate, the detail text box should be left blank when doing this first step. The bracketed range on the screen is a starting point to determine a reasonable detail strata size. The AI software selects $850 as a detail cutoff. The 97th percentile cutoff is $744 with a detail size of 314 records while the 99th percentile cutoff is $1,896 with detail size of 104 records. The AI decision is to make the **detail cutoff at $850**. It is left to the reader to vary several cutoffs to measure their effect on sample size. Also vary number of strata and precision. <u>Because financial data is so varied there is always room for human intervention to fine tune the final sample design.</u> Start with entering the $850 cutoff then click **"1. Sample Calculations"** with precision .04 and number strata 5 to obtain the sample design. Vary inputs as discussed next to see impact on sample size.

Stratification

The next variable to test is the number of strata. It is both detail cutoff
One variable to test is the number of strata. It is both detail cutoff and
number of strata that determine statistical efficiency. Vary both inputs
and determine their effect on sample size. Sampling efficiency is the
ratio of the variability (standard deviation) of the total audit population,
not stratified with the stratified sample design. For example a sample
efficiency of 84% means that a stratified sample with a detail cutoff
has 84% less variability or lower standard deviation than a non-
stratified simple random sample. When selecting the number of strata,
one should find the minimum number of strata that balances both
efficiency and sample size. For example if 5 strata and 6 strata have
approximately the same efficiency and sample size then condense to
the more compact lower value of 5.

Precision

Another important factor in determining sample size is precision or as
termed by pollsters, "margin of error". The usual way of expressing it
is to determine the sample size that would provide sample estimates
within a specified range of the true population value. Suppose we have
a book total value of $1000 and our goal is to have a sample estimate
within 3% (precision) of the true book value. This would be in the
range of $970 and $1030. Precision and confidence levels are generally
used together in estimating population values. A more accurate way of
expressing the relationship between precision and confidence is stating
one is 95% confident that sample results would be within 3% of the
true population value. In statistics 95% confidence means that 95 out
of 100 random samples would fall within the 3% precision. In
calculating sample size Auditmetrics uses the standard of 95%
confidence interval.

Sample size is primarily driven by three factors: the variability (standard deviation) of the population to be sampled and precision and number of strata including the detail stratum. A precision of 3% would require a larger sample size than the wider precision of 5%. As sample size increases so does statistical power. On the other hand increasing sample size results in increased cost of conducting the audit. Therefore, as one tests different inputs using Auditmetrics, the cost/sample size tradeoff would be a consideration.

Final Design and Efficiency Factor

This web cutdown version is an expedited way to understand the interplay of the various inputs in determining sample size. There are some rules of thumb to follow in assessing statistical efficiency. An acceptable efficiency should be $\geq .70$. Efficiency between 70 and 60 usually indicates a highly skewed population. To eliminate the effect of extreme skewness, increase the precision and/or increase the amount of dollars in the detail cutoff. The cutoff in itself reduces skewness. If an efficiency factor does not reach .60, the guidance of a statistician should be considered. It does not occur often but when we have observed this phenomenon, we found the audit population is usually bi-modal. Bi-modality means that two independent processes or populations are artificially combined into one. The recommended statistical solution is to separate the two populations and audit each separately. The statistical efficiency of the medical claims case study data is well beyond the 70% criterion representing a relatively balanced distribution.

After testing the sensitivity of the several inputs on sample size, the next step is to actually generate a sample by clicking "2. Generate Sample" and then "3. Sample Validation".

Validity Check

Statistical sample audits have an advantage over other types of random sampling environments. When health researchers test different models of disease prevention or treatment effectiveness, a statistical sample is used to estimate a population parameter that is generally unknown. Previously published research and statistical theory help guide the researcher. But with an audit the auditor selects samples from computerized accounting systems. Such accounting systems can automatically summarize account totals and breakdowns, therefore key population parameters are generally known. In the exhibit below the precision is 4%. Once the sample is drawn we can use that sample to estimate a known population value which happens to be the population we used to draw that sample.

Suppose the precision in designing an audit sample is set at 4%. one validity check would be to determine if an estimate derived from that sample does indeed fall within the 4% audit population true value.

Below is a design based on a detail of $850, 5 strata and a precision (margin of error) equaling 4% with the resulting strata boundaries and sample size of 763.

.Detail	850	0 - 49.99
No. Strata	5	50 - 124.99
Precision	.04	125- 199.99
Efficiency	0.84	200- 374.99
Total Sample	763	375-850
Sample Size Excel File		>850
Sample Validation Excel		

Potential Detail

2.Generate Sample ←

When button #3 is clicked, in addition to defining stratification boundaries on the upper display, population and sample specification are displayed on the lower screen:

Both population size (N) and sample size (n) are displayed. What pops up is a new *button #2* to generate a tab delimited text (.txt) and a comma separated (.csv) sample. The advantage of the csv file is that it can be directly read by Excel and immediately saved as a spreadsheet. These file types will be discussed in more detail later.

| 0 -49.99 |
| 50-124.99 |
| 125-199.99 |
| 200-374.99 |
| 375-850 |
| > 850 |

Population:

N	Mean	Total $
2872	25.11	72122
2328	81.43	189564.2
2799	156.05	436774.8
1674	248.25	415567.5
523	413.09	216045.6
284	2226.98	632463.7

Sample:

n	Mean	SD.	Total $
31	27.11	13.73	840
89	81.73	55.23	7274
94	161.92	20.94	15220
127	245.33	108.67	31157
138	419.38	310.69	57875
284	2226.98	2228.09	632464

Observed sample precision under 0.04

no need to resample

The last line in the exhibit indicates that the validity check has been passed. To see how this test is carried out, copy and paste this screen into an Excel spread sheet in order to conduct the appropriate analysis.

Mean-Per-Unit Projection

Copy and Paste the screens onto a spreadsheet. Use this spreadsheet to compare sample projected totals with the actual book total. What is needed are two columns titled "Sample Mean" and population frequency (**N**) then multiply Sample Mean X N. The input used for the sample size calculation was a 4% precision. Does the selected sample actually estimate an account total that is within the 4% target? The mean-per-unit method projects a total of $1,361,511 which is 2.47% within the actual total dollar volume of $1,330,074 and well below the 4% threshold.

Mean Per Unit Projection of Account Total

Population:		
N	Mean	Total $
2872	25.11	72,122
2328	81.43	189,564
2799	156.05	436,775
1674	248.25	415,567
523	413.09	216,046
284	2226.98	632,464
Actual Total-->		**$1,330,074**
Sample:		
Sample Mean		**N X Mean**
24.65		**$70,795**
87.11		**$202,792**
155.5		**$435,245**
252.09		**$421,999**
441.11		**$230,701**
"Not Sampled"		
Projected Total-->		**$1,361,531**

If one were to include the detail strata (284 transactions) to project the total dollar volume of the account from the sample, the observed precision would be 1.6%. In statistical terms, the detail is 35% of total dollar volume and is reviewed at 100% and does not involve statistical error and therefore results in a closer range around the true population value.

After the validity check on the screen is completed, a popup hyperlink, **"check sample stats"**, to another web page that compares the sample estimate of error rate with the population's actual error rate. Also included on the screen is a breakdown of the sample by the individual healthcare providers.

Population Error Rate:

Plan	total Amt.	Error Amt.	Rate
Acme	$1,962,538	$200,285	0.102

Actual Error Rate= .102

Sample Results:

Loc.	Sum	Error	Rate
HMO1	$575,936	$62,146	0.108
HMO2	$120,018	$8,384	0.07
MD	$52,534	$588	0.011

Sample Estimated Error: 0.105

The audit population actual error rate is 10.2% and the sample estimate is 10.5% in this run. Other samples may lead to different error rate estimates based on the luck of the draw of the random sample. The full Windows version of Auditmetrics does a second validity check that will be discussed later.

TPA claims processors would be very concerned if the error rate was ≥ 3%. Less than 3% is acceptable in private employer based health plans because there are usually time lags in the communication of company human resource departments concerning employee eligibility updates to health plan administrators and varying quality of medical office submission procedures. For publicly funded plans like Medicare there are a multitude of regulations that a health-care provider's billing system may miss. A knowledgeable accountant armed with a streamlined tool in conducting an audit has the best path for self-correction and self-protection.

A health plan's claims administrator provides feedback to both the plan member and healthcare provider. The plan member is sent an "explanation of benefits" statement that details all the claims paid and denied and what is the patient's cost responsibility. A similar report is sent to the healthcare provider. Being equipped with this feedback is one way for the auditor to have a path to enhancing an organization's knowledge of its administrative claims processing needs.

Quality management is the ability to anticipate. An auditor would be chagrined to realize there is a serious cash flow problem only after company cash flow needs cannot be met. It would be better to periodically obtain snapshots of current and recent activity that paves the way for solving problems when potential problems are relatively small. The same is true for assessing health plan administration and performance. At some point, an audit by an external agency may be mandated and that is not the time to start preparations. Large corporations have resources to afford experts and sophisticated software in-house. It is the mission of Auditmetrics and this provide a means of professional development and efficient administration that evens out the playing field for middle and small-sized firms.

Sample Break Downs

The case study was initially based on a variable sample based on the dollar value of each transaction. However once a sample is drawn and validated, the auditor then defines an attribute on the basis of a yes/no binomial decision in determining a claim error rate. This is also the methodology use in conducting a sales and use tax audit. However the sample can be used as a roadmap to study other relevant issue in terms of company performance. With a validated manageable account subset and with powerful Excel tools other attributes can and should be followed up.

In the claims case study there is an attribute breakdown, based on claims submitted from an HMO with two locations and doctors outside of the HMO network. As seen in error rate and dollar volume, HMO1 has the largest claims error rate. So, from a strategic perspective the auditor should start reviewing the administrative procedures at HMO1. Beginning the analytic process with HMO1 has the benefit of not only discovering its adequacies but also targeting where there is the greatest economic impact.

There can be other breakdowns of value that goes beyond administrative needs. The sample can also be useful in a preliminary market analysis. For example one may be interested in which employer plan dominates the patient pool of the HMO and specific gender and geographic characteristics can help in messaging and outreach. Comprehensive marketing research can be very sophisticated and a single variable sample as in this case study is only a start. It should be considered a first run uncovering marketing relevant attributes in terms of economic importance. It would also be valuable for an auditor to explore the fields of opinion polling and market research. Analysis in such studies involves the same basic statistical theory as applied in this book.

Excel is a useful tool for a number of marketing tasks. The most important is use as a tool for data analysis and reporting. The two most important tools is the use of **pivot tables** to arrange and categorize tabular data and how to create a histogram using the "**=FREQUENCY**" Function.

B. Auditmetrics Sales Tax Case Study

In this section will be discussed the use of the Windows Auditmetrics v 6.3 software. It would be best to follow the discussion with the software opening screen but if not able then review the computer screen exhibit on page 24.

The Supreme Court Wayfair decision has had a great impact on state and local revenue departments in accelerating the move toward using statistical methods in auditing for sales and use taxes. Because of that decision any state can tax internet sales in any other state. The previous law upended was that a business was exempt if it did not have a physical presence in a particular State. Internet sales can expand markets for any business but now with this decision there is a potential to be audited by 47 different states and there are also around 300 local sales tax authorities.

State auditing departments had been steadily moving in the direction of expanding the use of statistical audit techniques as promulgated by various groups like AICPA, IRS, and Multistate Tax Commission. The original impetus was when the IRS in 2009 developed statistical audit directives. Its view stated in its published directive is that: "*statistical sampling techniques are valuable examination tools where effective use of resources makes it uneconomical to audit voluminous accounting data. Proper use of statistical sampling substantially increases the quality of IRS examinations*". One can view update directive at the IRS web site. The Wayfair decision will only accelerate the move toward using statistical techniques.

There will be a need for academic institutions to reflect these growing trends in business accounting and auditing. There is also a trend for audits to be ongoing, analytical and semi-automate. *Auditmetrics* AI guidance will get small business up to speed when state revenue departments demand data for a statistical sample. It is our experience that most business are at a loss when enmeshed in such a technically based audit. The best protection for businesses is to prepare with their own internal statistical audits.

The software automatically generates two Excel spreadsheet templates, one will document the audit design and another can be used to record audit results. It has been my experience that accountants are very capable in using Excel. However to be effective, auditors also need to be adept in database manipulation. This is somewhat lacking for most auditors. Therefore appendix II covers Access as a database management resource.

1. Let's Get Started

Create on your computer a folder called Auditmetrics_Test and place the tab delimited file test_population.txt that came with your software. You can park your files of interest on any folder you wish to create. Click on the Auditmetrics icon to get started. Before calculating sample size you need three input values that are requested on the screen:

Detail Cutoff

The first step is to determine "detail stratum." This is the stratum in which one does not rely on a sample but a review of 100% of all transactions in that stratum. Eliminating the largest transactions from sampling enhances statistical efficiency in that the detail stratum allows a direct review of all transaction with the greatest economic impact.

To start, click on the tab **"Potential Detail Cutoff"**. AI will provide a value for detail cutoff. A rule of thumb is that the detail stratum should represent approximately 1/3 of total dollar volume but Auditmetrics uses a more statistical analytical approach and for this test dataset it is $7,500.

Also displayed are the upper percentile rankings of dollar volume. The auditor should initially spend time getting a sense of the distribution characteristics of the account to be audited. The auditor can vary detail cutoffs to determine if there is a more efficient input combination. The percentile rankings on the screen help in getting a sense of where the initial cutoff is located. As we cover the other inputs in determining proper sample size, you will find that you may get better results by tweaking all inputs.

> *Professional Version, Auditmetrics-AI, has a radio button in the upper right hand corner that allows the "Potential Detail Cutoff" tab to be used to display Benford Law's first digit and second digit assessment. It is a useful forensic accounting tool to detect possible fraud.*

You will also notice that what is also displayed is the interquartile range. This is the range of dollar amount that contains the middle 50% of the total audit population. Of the 25,152 transactions one half are between $14 and $205, 25% less than $14 and 25% above $205. This will give the auditor an additional detailed look of sample segments for possible errors or other potential problems. Each Segment may represent different products or services that require different benchmarks, staffing, marketing needs and monitoring methods in guiding performance.

Account sample Analysis depends on how well sample criteria are met once a sample is drawn. The random process can lead to a sample that does not produce estimates within the desired precision. That is the characteristic of randomness. The 95% confidence interval means it can occur 5% of the time. Auditmetrics–AI analytics guides you through the complex mathematics to test the sample's precision. If the standard is not met it is a simple matter to resample as was done in the case study.

The goal is to have a sample that meets established statistical standards. Yes, anyone can draw a random sample but will it hold up under scrutiny? Will it provide tightly focused statistical estimates or estimates that shows that it is an outlier?

A. The Number of Strata

Stratification is the process of dividing the population of transactions into segments (strata) based on a certain characteristic. In sampling based on dollars, stratification is based on the dollar amount of the transaction. A stratified random sample will yield more precise results than an unrestricted random sample of the same size. Six strata is a default but other values should be tested to test impact on sample size.

B. Precision

The default precision or margin of error on the screen is 3%. If the audit is for a formal submission to the IRS or state revenue agency, the precision gold standard should be 3%. If you are conducting an internal audit and just want to get a preliminary look at the data then choose less precise values such as 4% or 6%. These will result in a smaller sample size but sufficient to get a sense of the data.

Do a run with detail 7500 with precision and number of strata defaults. Then:

Explore the interaction of detail, precision and number of strata impact on sample size.

C. Efficiency Factor

 You should notice on the screen the measure "Efficiency Factor". If the efficiency factor of a particular dataset does not exceed 60% then it would be advisable to graph the dataset using Excel's the ="**frequency**" to create a histogram of the data or summarize the data with a pivot table.   It is valuable to get a picture of the data to decide the level of skewness or disjointed nature of the data. At times it may be advisable to separate the data to do separate analysis. If the data set is very large do a cutdown as was discussed previously then do the plotting or tabulations.

Once the three inputs are decided upon then select the "1. Sample Size Calculations" tab.

2. **Generating the Sample**

If the sample specifications displayed on the screen are acceptable, the next step is to generate the sample. Select tabs **"2. Select Random Sample"** and **"3. Sample Validation"** . That is all that is required and two random sample files will be generated: "SampleData.txt" and "SampleData.csv". The .csv file is a comma separated variable file which is a text file that can be directly read into Excel and saved as an Excel workbook. The .txt file uses a tab as a variable separator. Both files will be saved in the same folder that had originally been set up for the audit population data.

3. Validating the Sample

Once you are satisfied with the sample as displayed on the screen, then spreadsheet templates can be generated to document and record audit results. As part of deciding on a final design, does the actual precision of the randomly selected sample actually match the original targeted precision?

In the Medical claims case study we covered this first validity check. If the precision test fails then re-run "**1. Sample Size Calculation**" to start the process again. Redo steps 2 and 3 until the observed precision of the sample matches or is better than the precision used during sample design.

This is an overall sample validation based on precision, the next validation test is a strata by strata statistical test.

The second validation testis a pass/fail 95% confidence interval for each stratum. Its results will on the screen. If one or more strata fail then start again to calculate another sample and point and click until both validation test #1 and test #2 are passed.

Only Proceed when All strata are designated as indicated Below:

n	Mean	SD.	Total $		
69	22.74	22.78	1569	ok	ok
84	141.33	69.6	11871	ok	ok
89	418.15	174.03	37216	ok	ok
129	1001.66	404.51	129215	ok	ok
172	2108.62	955.52	362682	ok	ok
125	4412.92	2562.87	551614	ok	ok
451	30657.11	68197.67	13826355		

Validation #1- Observed precision under 0.03 no need to resample

Validation #2- Strata specific test passed.

4. Documenting the sample

After a specific sample design is decided upon, the next step is to document the sample in an Excel spreadsheet. You will now do one final run but this time it should be done with the following radio buttons selected.

The step are:

1. Select button **"1. Sample Size Calculation"** with:

• Sample Size Excel File
o Sample Validation Excel File

   Then **"2. Select Random Sample"** and **"3. Sample Validation"**. The sample calculation step will run again but this time generate an Excel file. It will document sample specs that should be shared with all interested parties.

2. Then again select button **"1. Sample Size Calculation"** **"2. Select Random Sample"** and **"3. Sample Validation"** now with:

o Sample Size Excel File
• Sample Validation Excel File

   At this stage a spreadsheet is generated that includes the strata specific statistical validation. In the section of the spreadsheet entitled "audit results", one can fill in the blank column **" amount error"** and an overall error rate and its 95% confidence interval be displayed. This is the default to determine such things as sales tax or medical claims dollars in error. There is no confidence interval around the detail projection because it is 100% of that stratum.

   For more discussion of the spreadsheet templates refer to Appendix I

The spreadsheet templates are protected so that you cannot inadvertently write over a critical formula. If you need to make alterations then go to review at Excel's top menu and select "unprotect sheet"

5. Data Mining as a Sequel

Auditmetrics gets you started in sampling an account based on dollars. In business, dollars are the life blood of survival. With its templates, Auditmetrics can determine which dollars do not meet sufficient performance, in both absolute and percentage terms. You may have noticed that when a political poll is discussed in addition to the overall percentage result, most will ask "what are the internals" of the poll. That means is how do the overall results relate to important breakdown factors such as gender, race, economic status and age. In statistics it is called crosstabs which exposes the underlying dynamics that help to plan future action. The original dollars is a quantitative variable while the factor breakdowns are attributes. This where the pivot table for breakdowns of the sample is very valuable

Below is excerpted from a random sample that an auditor used to monitor the supply chain for a small manufacturing company:

Transactio	amount	absamt	PERIOD	Vendor	Strata	Error
22	421.43	421.43	3/1/2017	Jones & Sons	3	yes
24351	550	550	2/1/2016	ACE Dist.	3	no
8585	51	51	4/1/2015	ABC Co.	1	no
12345	7000	7000	3/1/2015	Smith Bros.	5	no
24376	10500	10500	6/1/2017	Acme Inc.	6	yes
14666	6034.48	6034.48	1/1/2015	Acme Inc.	5	no
80	9000	9000	2/1/2017	Smith Bros.	6	no
	.	.	.	.	.	.
	.	.	.	.	.	.

In conducting the audit a record was kept by the auditor to monitor which transactions contained errors. It was determined if a delivery was incomplete, faulty, delayed, the wrong supply or price etc. All costly delays in doing business. The Auditmetrics sample and templates documents the scope of the problem. But more is needed to guide the auditor towards a solution.

Using an Excel pivot table the auditor can now target corrective measures. A true attribute percentage would be how many transaction are in error. The percentage displayed below is based on how many dollars are in error providing a more detailed economic impact statement.

Sum of amount	Error By Vendor			Percent Error
	Error ▾			
Company ▾	no	yes	Grand Total	By Vendor
ABC Co.	$3,880,847	$166,861	$4,047,708	4%
ACE Dist.	$1,548,288	$159,263	$1,707,552	9%
Acme Inc.	$3,391,568	$398,518	$3,790,085	11%
Flower Inc.	$1,701,054	$205,547	$1,906,601	11%
Jones & Sons	$1,696,507	$405,821	$2,102,328	19%
Smith Bros.	$1,656,511	$112,436	$1,768,947	6%
Grand Total	$13,874,774	$1,448,446	$15,323,221	

What does this mean for small business? We are entering a high tech commercial environment where huge commercial entities can marshal vast sophisticated programming to correct past deficiencies and search for potential opportunities. Auditmetrics helps the smaller enterprise to use accepted analytical tools that can fill in the void to survive in the modern economy.

6. Data Trouble Shooting

The dataset for analysis requires a rectangular matrix with each variable is a column and each individual transaction is a row. There are times when you think your data is all set for analysis and then you get the message:

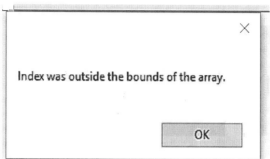

This is a message thrown off by the operating system and the usual problem is there is something wrong with the data. Processing cannot continue. What usually generates this error message is that the original Excel file contained blank lines (row 15414) with no data or only partial data (row 15430):

	A	B	C	D	F
	DataSet	Transaction ID	Account ID	Account Name	Amount
15413	ERG	15410	107691	Acme Co.	15
15414					
15415	ERG	15412	310789	XYZ Co.	35
15428	ERG	15425	107691	Acme Co.	45
15429	ERG	15426	310789	XYZ Co.	12
15430	Workshop				
15431	ERG	15427	107691	Acme Co.	25
15432	ERG	15428	310789	XYZ Co.	32
15433	ERG	15429	310789	XYZ Co.	15

Excel is a file manager not a database manager so when it is solely used as a data source, it may not be in the form of a rectangular data matrix with the columns as variables and rows as individual data records. In this case the blank and partial rows are throwing off the Auditmetrics data parser. Sorting the file will help in determine if each row is complete. See Appendix V for more detail

QuickBooks Excel Data Exercise

The latest version of Auditmetrics relies on standardized data for input and output. The data standard is text files of two types: .txt and .csv files. Auditmetrics data input is the tab delimited text file (.txt). Sample data output is both the tab delimited text file (.txt) and comma separated value file (.csv) which is also a text file. The .csv file has the advantage that it can be readily read in by Excel. It has all the functionality of a spreadsheet and immediately can be saved as a spreadsheet. Intuit QuickBooks operates in the small business market, sized at approximately 29 million businesses in the United States, and has more than 80% market share with small businesses that use financial management software. QuickBooks uses a "closed" database structure that you cannot access directly. If you want to extract transaction data, such as invoices or checks, you have to use a third party tool to extract data (or get the SDK/ programming toolkit and write your own program). An internet search will reveal several third party vendors to obtain data from QuickBooks.

Data for Auditmetrics should be at the transaction level in either a .csv or a tab delimited .txt file. These universal file structures make it possible to plugin data from QuickBooks standard reports *without the need for specialized software*. It works best with reports that detail data at the transaction level such as sales, expenses, accounts payable, accounts receivable etc. Reports that detail a summary at a sufficient detail is also useful. For example accounts receivables per customer (price x quantity) is a useful detail. Below is an example using a "Sales by Customer Report" in the Report section of QuickBooks.

Excel data files converted to text files are seamless as plugins to Auditmetrics. However most Excel spreadsheet reports are not specifically formatted as a rectangular data file. For example there are standard QuickBooks reports that can be exported to Excel. In this exercise **QuickBooks Desktop Pro** is used to export a "sales by customer report" from the sample learning database to ultimately create a plugin for Auditmetrics.

Below is a report with conversion options. **Select Excel**

Customize Rept.	Coment on Rept.	Share Template	Print	Email	Excel	Hide Header				
Sample Report									
	Type	**Date**	**Num**	**Name**	**Item**	**Qty**	**Amount**	**Balance**	
Ecker Design									
	Invoice	12/15/2021	131	Ecker D	Garde	1.00	1.00	1.00	
	Invoice	12/15/2021	131	Ecker D	Pest C	1.00	1.00	2.00	
Total Ecker Design						2.00	2.00	2.00	
Golliday									
75 Sunset Rd.									
	Invoice	12/02/2021	120	Gollida	Plants	10.00	10.00	10.00	
	Invoice	12/02/2021	120	Gollida	Install	54.00	54.00	64.00	
Total 75 Sunset Rd.						64.00	64.00	64.00	
Golliday Sporting G						64.00	64.00	64.00	
Heldt, Bob									
	Invoice	12/08/2021	123	Heldt, I	Plants	2.00	2.00	2.00	
------------>	Invoice	12/08/2021	123	Heldt, I	Plants	3.00	3.00	5.00	
	Invoice	12/08/2021	123	Heldt, I	Fertili	6.00	6.00	11.00	

Auditmetrics Data Input

The QuickBooks Report menu bar drop-down list has an option to generate Excel files. One can either generate a new file or add to an existing file. The problem with exporting to a standard report Excel worksheet is it will have the same layout as a printed report hardcopy. Invoice data are embedded and not readily reachable as data elements for processing by Auditmetrics. There is a Report option that will help in selecting invoice data. Once you select the Excel option you are then asked to where to send the report. Select the last option to create a .csv text file.

Send Report to Excel

Would you like to do with this Report?

o   Create a new worksheet

o   Update an existing worksheet

o   Replace an existing worksheet

·   **Create a comma separated values (.csv) file**

The Report option in this exhibit is not to generate a worksheet but to obtain a .csv file which is a text file readable by Excel. It may look like an ordinary spreadsheet but it is a special text file that can be manipulated and used to create a rectangular text file that can be plugged into Auditmetrics.

Below is the QuickBooks Excel spreadsheet report converted to a .CSV text file:

Type	Date	Num	Name	Amount
Crenshaw, Bob				
Invoice	12/10/2021	FC 8	Crenshaw, Bob	$60.00
Total Crenshaw, Bob				
DJ's Computers				
Invoice	12/15/2021	132	DJ's Computers	$125.00
Total DJ's Computers				
Ecker Design				
Invoice	12/15/2021	131	Ecker Design	$23.00
Invoice	12/15/2021	131	Ecker Design	$68.00
Total Ecker Design				

You can use Excel to read in the .csv text file and now it is easy to manipulate. **Sort the .CSV file by Type and Date.**

Type	Date	Num	Name	Amount
Invoice	12/10/2021	FC 8	Crenshaw, Bob	$60.00
Invoice	12/15/2021	132	DJ's Computers	$125.00
Invoice	12/15/2021	131	Ecker Design	$23.00
Invoice	12/15/2021	131	Ecker Design	$68.00
Crenshaw, Bob				
Total Crenshaw, Bob				
DJ's Computers				
Total DJ's Computers				
Ecker Design				
Total Ecker Design				

All of the invoices are bunched together and now it is a simple matter to remove all extraneous rows and come up with a **true rectangular dataset ready for analysis**.

Add Auditmetrics Required Variables:

Amount, Absamt, Transaction_ID and DataSet.

Num	Amount	Absamt	Transaction_ID	DataSet
131	($23.00)	$23.00	3	Run_1
FC 8	$60.00	$60.00	1	Run_1
131	$68.00	$68.00	4	Run_1
132	$125.00	$125.00	2	Run_1

The highlighted columns in gray are required variables for an Auditmetrics text file. Amount was already part of the QuickBooks dataset. But added are three other required variables Absamt, Transaction_ID, and DataSet. These variable names are required:

1. **Amount** – The transaction of interest in the analysis.
2. **Absamt** – Absolute value of each transaction. The data set <u>must</u> be sorted in an ascending order. This is to handle credits.
3. **Transaction_ID** – an identifier for each record, it is a record count.
4. **DataSet** – A name to identify this specific dataset.
5. **Primary Key Optional** – If a dataset is from a relational database with a primary key that links the various data tables it is prudent to include this variable in the audit population dataset to be sampled.

Variables 1 to 4 names must be in the data file and spelled exactly as above, letter case and order do not matter. If not present, Auditmetrics will reject the file. The same is true if Absamt is not sorted in ascending order.

If you need to add or create other variables it is safest to use letters and numbers with no embedded spaces. For example if you want to name a variable Run 1 It is best to use Run _1 or Run1. This is rule true for many data base and statistical software.

Transaction_ID has value especially when the data set is the merging of several data sources. For example, if you have two data sets of 1000 each and use MS Access to merge them then Transaction_ID 1 to 1000 are from the first dataset and 1001 to 2000 are from the second dataset. Transaction_ID also has value when filing with the IRS. For more details review Appendix III – Random Sampling and IRS Directives

<u>The worksheet is now ready to be "saved as" a tab delimited .TXT</u>
Comma variable separated (.csv) files are standard text files for data transfer but for Auditmetrics only Tab delimited file are required input because for many .csv files commas are embedded in many fields such as the "Name" field listed below:

Name
Williams, Abraham
Rummens, Suzie
Heldt, Bob
Crenshae,Bob
Hughs, Davis

In the standard Quickbooks report, the name variable is last name comma first name. This comma is not a variable separator and if left in place, would distort the dataset. Auditmetrics uses **only tab delimited .txt files as data input**. Prior versions of Auditmetrics did allow .csv files for input but it required two passes of the data one to cleanse stray commas and then use the clean file for data plug-in. It may not be a problem for small data sets but with a book of five million transactions it does take a toll on operational efficiency and no matter how complete the cleansing software, stray commas may sneak in. Therefore it was decided to use only tab delimited files for input.

Best Data Practices

When getting data from many different sources, to be safe, numerical data for analysis in Excel should be formatted as "general" format not currency or other numerical formats that imbed other characters such as commas, dollar signs and parenthesis. Auditmetrics data parser is powerful and can handle a wide variety of accounting formats but the problem may arise when several different data sources are used and each may have its own individual quirk.

If you are deriving a tab delimited file from a MS Access query using amount and absamt as currency is fine for Auditmetrics. But if you want to interface with other software then make sure the table, from which the query is built has amount and absamt set as data type "number" <u>Also define the format as field size "double" format</u> <u>"general number" and "decimal places" as 2.</u> Review Appendix II for details about deriving data from an Access database.

Detail Revisited

A. Skewness and Risk

The detail stratum is an effective way of minimizing statistical error. Financial data tends to be skewed with most transactions clustered together but with a few at a high dollar value. Skewness risk in financial modeling is when observations are dramatically asymmetric. It can create statistical estimation problems. The value of a 100% review of the detail stratum accomplishes two distinct positives. Economically the transactions with the greatest economic impact are reviewed without any sampling error. It is what it is. Another benefit is the variability and potential statistical error of the remaining transactions is greatly reduced. Therefore projections derived from the non-detail strata would have smaller confidence interval ranges as compared to an analysis where all transaction are subject to statistical error.

B. The External Audit

Many businesses are subject to an external agent coming in to examine their books. For example, a state revenue department may audit the books of a business regarding sales tax payments or lack thereof. Doctors and hospitals are also subject to such reviews when third party payers such as the government or insurance companies audit past paid health insurance claims. The summary of the audit is usually expressed as a total error rate.

Too often the government or other outside agent comes in, asks for records for a year or more, draws a sample and then sends a bill sometimes involving thousands or tens of thousands of dollars. Other sanctions may be imposed such as fines or a requirement that all staff attend education workshops at employer expense, a Federal government favorite. The first line of defense is preemptive in-house reviews and to set targets for performance. Such reviews can indicate if account transactions conform to existing law and/or accepted practice. It also can aid in identifying faulty internal control procedures. Anyone can draw a random sample but the issue is can that sample stand up to scrutiny in terms of precision and confidence level?

C. The Internal Audit

The internal audit has a dynamic with additional burdens. Suppose the auditor designs a sample for sales data with 6 strata and a detail cutoff of $20,000. The internal auditor's goal is not to just measure a total error rate but to examine issues such as operational inefficiency or other failures that may not show up on a system standard report. This is where the internal auditor can head off incipient problems. Management excellence is when one anticipates problems before they become obvious.

Each stratum may reflect different market segments with its own operational control needs. A stratum with product prices under $10 would have a different dynamic than a stratum containing items in the range of thousands of dollars. Each may require different benchmarks, staffing, marketing needs and monitoring methods in guiding performance. Strata subsets should be individually examined. In the medical claims case study, an overall error rate was uncovered but upon further examination it was found that one particular HMO had an exceptionally high error rate. This is the detective work an internal auditor must explore. The audit is in not in a vacuum. There are usually standard reports that may point to an initial sampling which in turn may lead to potential follow-up sampling.

Auditmetrics displays an overall precision validity check, but it is a first step in examining the total sample. But the auditor must look into the validity of each stratum. In this context a strata by strata validation is also important. You will notice that the Auditmetrics validation Excel spreadsheet has a pass/fail designation for each stratum using a 95% confidence interval. If a stratum fails the test then one should go back to the sample calculation button and proceed until all validation tests are passed, both the overall precision and strata specific 95% confidence interval test.

Forensic Accounting using Benford's Law

Benford's Law provides a data analysis method that can help alert CPAs to possible errors, potential fraud, manipulative biases, costly processing inefficiencies or other irregularities. It is a relatively simple formula:

$$p(d) = Log_{10}(1/(1+d))$$

Benford's Law gives the expected patterns of the digits in the numbers tabulated. Those digits, in unaltered data, will not occur in equal proportions; there is a large bias towards the lower digits, so much so that nearly one-half of all numbers are expected to start with the digits 1 or 2. The widespread applicability of Benford's Law and its practical use is to detect fraud, errors and other anomalies. There are many examples on the internet of authentic and accurate data that conforms to Benford's Law – and the fraudulent and invented numbers that do not.

The professional version of Auditmetrics-AI has an added feature that when you determine the cutoff for Detail strata you can also do a Benford's first and second digit test. It will also does a goodness of fit chi square test to determine whether the data set being analyzed statistically conforms to the Benford formula.

This explanation also suggests some important considerations when performing investigations using Benford's Law. One is that the law applies only to naturally occurring data. Purchase amounts, payment amounts, stock prices, accounts payable data, inventory prices and customer refunds are all good examples of such data. It is important to avoid using financial data that are not natural. For example, the purchases at a discount store might not lend themselves to Benford analysis, because there are limited price points per item. Similarly, values with upper and lower limits, such as maximum or minimum allowed values.

Non-natural numbers when aggregated can be considered natural numbers, For example a restaurant's menu has set prices for specific items. Not considered a generated list of natural numbers. However, when a total bill of all items is compiled into a total invoice, which is a sum of price x quantity, this can be considered a naturally generated set of numbers.

It is important to sample "fairly" when selecting a set of data for analysis. For example, limiting a sample of invoices to values between US $100 and US $999 defeats the tests because the data are limited to a narrow range. For small companies, using the complete data for an entire month is a better option.

Finally, as a technical matter, it is important to obtain a set of test data that is large enough to obtain useful statistical results. Auditmetrics-AI uses chi-square test which compares expected observations based on Benford to what is actually observed.

When Benford Analysis Is Likely Used	*Examples*
Sets of numbers that result from mathematical combination of numbers – Result comes from two distributions	*Accounts receivable (number sold * price), Accounts payable (number bought * price)*
Transaction-level data	Disbursements, sales, expenses

On large data sets – The more observations, the better	Full year's transactions ideal
Accounts that appear to conform – When the mean of a set of numbers is greater than the median and the skewness is positive	Most sets of accounting numbers fit this pattern
When Benford Analysis Is Not Likely Used	**Examples**
Data set is comprised of assigned numbers	Check numbers, invoice numbers, zip codes
Numbers that are influenced by human thought	Prices set at psychological thresholds ($1.99, ATM withdrawals
When Benford Analysis Is Not Likely Used (cont.)	**Examples**
Accounts with a large number of firm-specific numbers	An account specifically set up to record $100 or more refunds
Accounts with a built in minimum or maximum	Set of assets that must meet a threshold to be recorded
Where no transaction is recorded	Thefts, kickbacks, contract rigging

Benford Example

Below is an Auditmetrics-AI display of both a first and second digit Benford analysis of an account. Clearly the observed pattern deviates considerably from the Benford pattern:

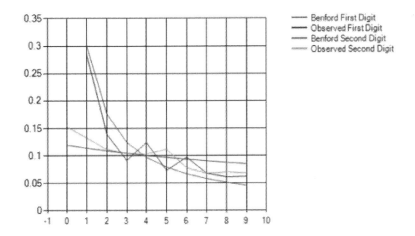

As can be seen the actual observed patterns for both first and second digit are considerably different from Benford's Law. But is it fraud. If you examine the pattern there are spikes at 4 and 6 for the first digit. There is no spiking for the second digit but a clear observable deviation.

What could be the explanation? If there was a special promotion with a sale price of $4.60 with a high customer demand then there is no indication of fraud. However this data is from an actual fraud case. The data is from an accounts payable file as an aggregate per supplier total. The auditor decided to probe further and found there was unusual high variable activity by one specific individual with a specific supplier. It turned out there was a sham supplier where payments were sent.

The reason not readily observable was that the fraud was conducted carefully, periodically varying days and weeks and varying dollar amounts small enough to be not to be noticed over a long period of time, well hidden in the shadows. But the auditor collected data over a long period of time and with a large volume of observations the pattern emerged. Numbers under Benford follow logarithmic patterns, fortunately fraudsters do not think in that same pattern and cannot generate logarithmic patterned numbers.

Auditmetrics – AI uses Goodness of fit Chi Square to test the observed account data distribution with the that as defined by Benford's formula.

First Digit Chi Square Results p <.05:

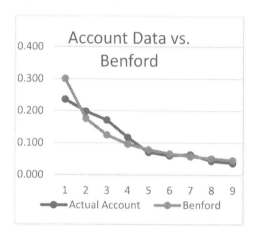

The best way to determine Benford compliance is to look at the plots of the data. It is the spike point that may be the first indictor of potential fraud.

Repeated cycles of audits using statistical methods assure both the auditor and the client that in the long run accumulated sample derived knowledge base would be identical to, or in mathematical terms, converge onto the true book value

Appendix I – Generating Excel Templates

This screen is almost identical to the internet version. The difference is two radio buttons that when selected generate an Excel workbook to document the sample design (Sample Size Excel file) and document sample validation and results of the audit (sample validation Excel).

| • Sample Size Excel File |
| o Sample Validation Excel File |

If you select "1. Sample Size Calculation" with radio button "Sample Size Excel File" following spreadsheet is generated:

HealthPlan1					
Strata:	Sample Size	Mean	Std. Dev.	Total Value	Pop. Total
0-49.99	31	$25.11	$15	$72,122	2,872
50-124.99	89	$81.43	$50	$189,564	2,328
125-199.99	94	$156.05	$42	$436,775	2,799
200-374.99	127	$248.25	$91	$415,567	1,674
375-850	138	$413.09	$304	$216,046	523
>850	284	$2,226.98	$0	$632,464	284
Totals Including Detail	763			$1,962,538	10,480
Sampling Efficiency	0.84				

This spreadsheet documents the population mean, standard deviation, total dollars by strata and frequency. The first column indicates the sample size by each stratum.

If you try various combinations of detail, precision and number of strata and are satisfied with what is displayed on the screen then before selecting **"3. Sample Validation"** select:

o	Sample Size Excel File
•	Sample Validation Excel File

What is generated is a spreadsheet that captures both population and sample documentation. This spreadsheet is structured so you can use it to summarize audit results. With the input of the medical claims case study.

What is displayed is from the *sample section* of the spreadsheet. For each strata is indicated that the validity test has been passed. The column "Amount Error" is filled in by the auditor after totaling those transactions from the sample that are in error. The spreadsheet contains all of the Excel formulas to calculate the 95% confidence interval around the sample estimate of $33,500 of taxes owed. It should be noted that the 95% confidence interval displayed is a one sided confidence interval **which is consistent with IRS directives.**

Sample		Audit Results	Validity Check
Sample Total Value	Sample Size	Amount Error	
$1,011	41	$28	pass
$7,636	89	$225	pass
$14,486	94	$436	pass
$31,217	127	$916	pass
$58,512	138	$152	pass
$632,464	284	$6,325	
$112,861	489		
$745,325	773		
		Sample Error Rate =	0.025
		Overall Rate=	0.020
Detail Error	$6,325		
Sample Estimate:			
Lower Bound	$33,110		
Mid-Point	$33,500		
Upper Bound	$33,891		

Appendix II – Tab Delimited plugin from MS Access

Microsoft Access is a versatile relational database system. A relational database (RDB) is a collective set of multiple data sets organized by tables. RDBs establish a well-defined relationship between database tables. Tables communicate and share information, which facilitates data search ability, organization and reporting. The dataset for medical claims was derived from an Access based claims processing system. The table selected is a subset of a much larger dataset with personal identifiers removed and non-standard medical procedure codes specifically set-up for this exercise. Care was taken to assure compliance with the Health Insurance Portability and Accountability Act (HIPAA) privacy standards.

Paid Claim MS Access table design:

PaidClaims <---Table Name	
Field Name	Data Type
Transaction_ID	Number
amount	Number
PlanName	Text
End_Coverage	Text
ServDate	Text
Error	Text
Service_Location	Text
Procedure Code	Text

This table was set up with Auditmetrics variables amount and Transaction_ID and Transaction_ID should be an "AutoNumber or a count of each transaction. Please note amount is also data type "Number", a more complete format listing for amount should be field size "double" and decimal places 2. If the data comes from a relational database there may be a primary key that integrates several tables. This also should be included as a separate variable so that the sample can be integrated with other tables.

For the data needs of Auditmetrics what is also needed is absamt, absolute value for amount and sorted into ascending order. What also is required is the variable DataSet to identify this particular data for export. To do this you need to set up a Query.

If you are not comfortable in setting up an Access table and related query, an internet search will reveal many sites that demonstrate how. At this juncture we have a table which contains the claims data. In order to add the two variables (absamt and Dataset) a query will be required. A query is a database object that creates a datasheet of specified records from one or more tables. A query allows an analysis of the data from different perspectives.

Claims Data Query

	Paid Claims Table		
Procedure_Code	absamt: Abs([amount])	DataSet: "HPlan1"	
PaidClaims			
	Ascending ←		

This exhibit is a segment of the query that contains all of the table variables plus two added variables required by Auditmetrics. Absamt is created with the script **absamt:Abs([amount]).**

In a query any text followed by a colon indicates that this is a new variable. After the colon the script indicates exactly what is the value of the new variable. In this instance it is the absolute value of the table variable amount. You should also note that absamt is sorted in ascending order. <u>Be sure you use the query to sort absamt.</u> The second required variable is DataSet and designated by the script **DataSet:"HPlan1"**. In this case the new variable has a single value HPlan1. What follows is a listing of the query:

Query1				
R	R	R	R	
Transaction_ID	amount	absamt	DataSet	Serv_Loc
96	9.95	9.95	HlthP1	HMO1
263	10	10	HlthP1	HMO1
260	10	10	HlthP1	HMO2
203	10	10	HlthP1	HMO1
284	10	10	HlthP1	HMO1
185	10	10	HlthP1	MD-Office
183	10	10	HlthP1	HMO2
235	10	10	HlthP1	MD-Office

The data is now in the form required by Auditmetrics. The "R" at the top indicates the specific variables required. Now the next step is to obtain a tab delimited .txt file that can be read-in by Auditmetrics.

I Select External Data & Text File

At this point go to the main Access menu bar at the top and select "External Data" tab then "Export" and under file selections select text file. The first screen pop-up will ask some formatting questions you should ignore. Just move to the next screen by selecting OK. The next screen will ask what type file format you want to use. **Choose delimited.**

II Select Delimited then select Next.

O	Delimited - Comma or tab separate each field **<--------**
O	Fixed Width - Fields aligned in Columns with Spaces Between

Sample export format

1	96	9.95	9.95	HlthP1	HMO1
2	98	10.95	10.95	HlthP1	HMO1

III Select the actual delimiter, in this example "Tab" and also include field names on first row and text qualifier as {none} then save the file with and extension of .txt for tab delimited or .csv for coma separated. **<u>Be sure Text Qualifier is {none}.</u>**

Choose The Tab delimiter that separates your fields

Tab •	Semicolon 0	Comma 0	Space 0	Other 0

include Field Names in First Row

Text Qualifier {none}

Make sure you do these three selections, omitting any one can cause problems in the processing.

Appendix III

IRS Sliding Confidence Intervals

The IRS has developed a unique sliding scale confidence interval. Contact us at info@auditmetrics.com *for a worksheet that documents the formulas.*

With the current economy and its uncertainty, companies are taking advantage of federal tax credits and deductions to generate much needed cash. Claiming these credits and deductions often requires detailed review of large amounts of data. Statistical sampling is a useful tool in making a very large task manageable and is an even more cost effective solution now under the statistical sampling guidance issued by the Internal Revenue Service.

Statistical sampling is used both by taxpayers and the IRS as a tool for the estimation and the examination of various numbers that appear on a tax return or claim for a refund. There has been a substantial rise in taxpayer use of statistical sampling since the IRS First issued its field directives.

Some of the areas in which sampling has been particularly helpful include:

- Producing estimates of qualified research expenditures for purposes of calculating the research credit.

- Estimating the amount of meal and entertainment expenses misclassified to accounts that are only 50-percent deductible.

- Generating figures for fixed-asset additions that can be depreciated over shorter useful lives.

- Reclassifying capitalized amounts as currently deductible repairs. Assisting in the determination of a taxpayer's domestic production deduction

- The IRS has been using sampling for decades to examine many areas of tax return supporting data that are too voluminous to approach with any other technique.

Over the years, as the IRS has become more familiar with sampling concepts and the evaluation and use of statistical samples, it also has become more sophisticated in its approach. In November 2002, the IRS demonstrated its commitment to sampling by creating sampling coordinator positions. Sampling coordinators are responsible for communicating sampling's benefits, writing guidance and training materials, achieving nationwide consistency in application, and expanding the IRS's sampling knowledge and capabilities.

The IRS Shortcoming

It is the opinion of Auditmetrics the original 2002 statistical sampling directive treated statistical precision ranges in a total punitive manner. We will explain in a future continuing education newsletter our assessment of the punitive nature of the original 2002 directive.

The specific wording of the directive: "Taxpayer uses the least advantageous 95% one-sided confidence limit. The "least advantageous" confidence limit is either the upper or lower limit that results in the least benefit to the taxpayer." Confidence limit is the range that an estimate from a sample will actually contain the true population value that is too voluminous to measure directly. Associated with confidence limit is the concept of precision. Sometimes, as in polling, it is also referred as margin of error. We are exposed to this term constantly when following the rise and fall of political candidates. For example a pundit may say that the poll currently being discussed has a margin of error of 3%. You may have a point estimate for candidate A as 51%, with Candidate B at 49%. The margin of error states that the range is accurate up to 3% plus or minus around the 51%. The observed difference between the two candidates is only 1% so it would be declared "too close to call"

The plus or minus amount is used to create a confidence interval from 48 to 54 percent as a probable range of the estimate of all Americans who approve candidate A's performance. If the pollster were to use the IRS specification of the "least advantageous limit" the estimate would be the lower bound, 48%. Of course this does not make sense in polling but when estimating dollars it does, but in a negative way. By the way the confidence in the 90% confidence interval means that we are 90% confident that the true total population approval for candidate A is within the boundaries of 48 and 54 percent. Political pundits don't get into that level specificity.

The least advantageous limit does have economic consequences when estimating dollars. If you are estimating a $1,000,000 research tax credit from a sample that has a precision (margin of error) of 12% then the confidence interval would be between $1,120,000 and $880,000. Statistically the point estimate and most probable value of the true book value for a tax credit is $1,000,000 but the IRS will allow only $880,000 which has a decided economic impact. Sometimes the use of the lower bound is also referred to as the **taxpayer taking a haircut.**

The exhibit below outlines the impact using the least advantageous estimate to the taxpayer:

2002 IRS Statistical Audit Directive		
Upper Bound	1,120,000	
Sample Estimate	1,000,000	
Lower Bound	880,000	Taxpayer Haircut

Directive Updates

Though there is a recent IRS publication on statistical sampling the 2009/2011 directives started the process and did not place limitations on the types of issues that may be addressed through sampling. Rather, the taxpayer only must demonstrate that the use of sampling is appropriate, i.e., by showing that the burden of evaluating the necessary data without sampling would be high and that other books and records do not independently exist that would better address the particular issue. In practice, the IRS typically does not challenge the use of statistical sampling per se. The directives now allow:

- Forgiveness of the sampling error "haircut" when the precision is 10 percent or less. For example, if the estimate produced by the sample is $1 million and the associated sampling error is $100,000 (10%) or less, the taxpayer may claim the full benefit of $1 million without any reduction or taxpayer Haircut.

- Phase-in of the sampling error haircut when the precision is greater than 10% and less than 15%, the taxpayer would be allowed to phase in sampling error haircut over the range of 10 percent to 15 percent on a sliding scale. Assume the sampling error is $120,000, or 12% of the $1 million estimate. New IRS policy introduces a sliding scale, so the reduction to the tax benefit is not that large for sample estimates that just miss the 10-percent goal by a modest amount.

- **Inclusion of any certainty (detail) strata in the calculation of relative precision.**

  The last bullet is probably the most useful in estimating a tax credit with maximum benefit to the taxpayer. It is beyond the scope of this discussion but Auditmetrics has written a manual that goes into great detail how to assure a precision that maximizes benefits from the sample. The exhibit below gives three possible scenarios:

Scenario 1 if Rel. Precision <=10%	10%	
Upper Bound	1,100,000	
Sample Estimate (Allowed Credit)	1,000,000	No Taxpayer Haircut
Lower Bound	900,000	
Scenario 2 Rel. Precision >10% and <=15%	12%	
Upper Bound	1,120,000	
Sample Estimate	1,000,000	
Allowed Credit	952,000	Sliding Scale Haircut
Lower Bound	880,000	
Scenario 3 Rel. Precision >= 15%	15%	
Upper Bound	1,150,000	
Sample Estimate	1,000,000	
Lower Bound (Allowed Credit)	850,000	Tax Payer Haircut

As can be seen in scenario 2 the sliding scale allows for a tax credit of 952,000 just $48,000 below the maximum credit of $1,000,000.

Concluding remarks

We are well aware that just keeping up with tax law and your business day to day needs is time consuming enough. But the trend in using statistical methods is on the rise and will not abate. To ignore this trend as too lofty and not important for you and your clients will eventually leave you with a blind spot in maximizing benefits for your clients.

The IRS boosting the use of the statistical sample is part of a universal trend in using more and more sophisticated methods to enhance all types of analyses. Due to the explosion of information technology, what was once considered exotic is becoming common place. At one time our work in statistics revolved around complex statistical software but now much of what we did with our insider knowledge can be handled with Excel. That has caused a trend of converting a closed system of insider knowledge into a much more open ended system with broad availability and knowledge of, in this book, statistical methods.

The statistical sample can also expand an accountant's service line and statistical audits can be a good starting point. But it is a tool where the IRS has set up very specific standards. For example if you want the taxpayer to avoid a haircut then make sure the precision of the sample is less than 10%. Auditmetrics does that for you.

The primary driver of precision is sample size. But that is a double edged sword. The larger the sample size the better the precision but also the greater the cost of analyzing sample results.

Auditmetrics has written a step by step approach on the subject of designing a sample size that assures sufficient precision to avoid a taxpayer haircut. Included in this book is an appendix that provides a real world example that starts with an initial data set of approximately 10,000 records contained in an Excel Workbook. Using only Excel worksheet commands, it runs through the process from beginning to end in setting up the final calculation of sample size. The sample size is one that exhibits the necessary statistical power to meet the 3% margin of error gold standard. It be emphasized that the exercise in the appendix is for education purposes. Auditmetrics has automated that process for ease of implementation.

Appendix IV – Random Sampling Using Excel

Sample Selection - Excel based on IRS Directives

Recently the Internal Revenue Service has promoted the use of and published specific requirements concerning the statistical audit. We have published a summary of the IRS promotion for the use of statistical projections. The premise of this manual is that Excel is a useful aid in carrying out the statistical audit. However, there are two thorny issues regarding the use of Excel. One, it can be very cumbersome when dealing with very large data sets. We have discussed this in our Working Smart series. The second is, does Excel conform to random sample selection standards as published by the Internal Revenue Service?

IRS Specifications for Random Sampling

A random sample using Excel in accordance with IRS Directives has to be carefully designed and explained. The specific wording of the pertinent IRS directive is:

Taxpayers must retain adequate documentation to support the statistical application, sample unit findings, and all aspects of the sample plan and execution. The execution of the sample must be documented and include information for each of the following:

(1) The seed or starting point of the random numbers;

 (2) The pairing of random numbers to the frame along with supporting information to retrace the process;

(3) List of the sampling units selected and the results of the evaluation of each unit;

(4) Supporting documentation such as notes, invoices, purchase orders, project descriptions, etc., which support the conclusion reached about each sample item;

(5) The calculation of the projected estimate(s) to the population, including the computation of the standard error of the estimate(s);

(6) A statement as to any slips or blemishes in the execution of the sampling procedure and any pertinent decision rules; and

(7) Computation of all associated adjustments. (An example of an associated adjustment would be the amount of depreciation allowable based on a probability determination of an amount capitalized).

Items 2-7 deal with the linking of random numbers to the book of accounts, proper documentation and estimate methodology. With Auditmetrics CAATS each transaction in the audit population is assigned a "Transaction_ID" and when a sample is selected each transaction in the sample has the Transaction_ID to link back to the audit population.

Pseudorandom Process

A random sample of a book of transactions is a process whereby each transaction has an equal probability of being selected and forms what is referred to as the uniform distribution. A true random process is one in which each selected item does not predict or have influence on the next item to be selected. For example, if you go to a casino and play roulette, each number that comes up is totally independent of those that have preceded it.

However, using a true random process would be a very cumbersome. In the age of computer technology, it is very helpful and time saving if we design a computer algorithm to generate a series of random numbers that follow the uniform distribution. A starting point is to link a series of random numbers to a book of transactions. One standard way is to use an algorithm that starts with a seed number to generate a series of random numbers. For example, in the past we have used the millesecond reading from the computer's clock as a seed to generate a set of random numbers. The selection of the seed number in this instance is also a random process. This method can be more properly defined as a pseudorandom process.

A pseudorandom sequence of numbers exhibits statistical randomness while being generated by an entirely predictable mathematical process. Such a convenient methodology has the added benefit that with the same seed number one can produce exactly the same set of numbers. This is of value when sharing results with the IRS or other reviewers. With the same seed number, all parties can replicate the same random sample.

All major statistical software products such as SAS or STATA offer random processes with an option to use a seed number. But some software such as Excel and Auditmetrics do not. Auditmetrics offers a work around. The value of the seed number is for all parties to have the same random number sequence attached to a given set of transactions. Auditmetrics random sampling frame is stratified random sampling which is a very efficient method of sampling. The seed number criteria listed above would make documentation cumbersome by requiring a seed number for each stratum and segmenting the book of transactions to match each stratum. Auditmetrics links all sample items to audit population items so that all parties can examine the same set of data, i.e. the flow from the total book to sample.

An example using Excel

Microsoft documentation states that Excel's RAND function is seeded using the "system time" of the computer without much additional elaboration. Using a specific seed number is not possible. To get around this the first step is to link each transaction to a unique identifier. MS Access has a field format "AutoNumber" which numbers each transaction from "1" for the first record and incrementally up to the total number of the transactions. You can also accomplish this in Excel. For example if the first data point in column A1 is set at 1, then the second data point A2 is set A1+1. Then paste cell A2 to the end of the list of transaction in column A. Once that is done copy all of the transactions in the A column and paste special them in the same column as values.

93

Step 1: Set up Account Transaction ID

As previously discussed crate a transaction ID that uniquely identifies each individual transaction. <u>Be sure it is stored as a value and not in the formula form.</u>

ID	Amount	and. Numk
1	$2.00	=RAND()
2	$27.99	Etc.
3	$5.00	.
Etc.	$39.99	.
.	$39.99	.
.	$27.99	.
.	$5.00	.

Step 2: Generate Random Numbers

Use the formula **"=Rand()"** to generate a random number in a range between 0 and 1. In this example we want to sample 5 records from a population of 16.

Step 3: Copy Formula to all of the Transactions

ID	Amount	Rand. Numb.
1	$2.00	0.427605523
2	$27.99	0.08021559
3	$5.00	0.633252842
4	$39.99	0.847478392
5	$39.99	0.520001836

94

Step 4: Copy and Paste Random Numbers

With Excel every time you make changes to the spread sheet it also generates a new set of random numbers. This defeats the purpose of the seed number. By using the __paste / value option__ you convert the random sequence to an **unchangeable set of values**. You now have a column with a single set of random numbers tied to a single transaction. This fulfills the use of a seed number in that you have the ability to generate the same random sample:

ID	Amount	Rand. Numb.
1	$2.00	0.427605523
2	$27.99	0.08021559
3	$5.00	0.633252842
4	$39.99	0.847478392
5	$39.99	0.520001836

Step 5: Select Your Random Sample

Now sort your dataset in ascending order of your random number column.

ID	Amount	Rand. Numb.
15	$24.95	0.034160693
7	$5.00	0.037375766
11	$5.00	0.039393253
8	$27.99	0.164479651

1	$2.00	0.263221827
4	$39.99	0.264010164
9	$5.00	0.29091256
3	$5.00	0.312633768
6	$27.99	0.580692169
12	$1.29	0.62638731
2	$27.99	0.632090533
5	$39.99	0.729794316
14	$1.00	0.820569679
13	$1.29	0.867714912
16	$24.95	0.94713915
10	$24.95	0.953753009

You now have all transactions in a random order. You can take the first 5, last 5 or middle 5 records for a sample of size n=5. Just keep track of your decision rule.

Step 6: Sample n=5

ID	Amount	Rand. Numb.
15	$24.95	0.034160693
7	$5.00	0.037375766
11	$5.00	0.039393253
8	$27.99	0.164479651
1	$2.00	0.263221827

Stratified Random Sampling Using Excel

Our prior example outlines how to select a simple random sample. As has been mentioned previously, stratification enhances the efficiency of estimating parameters form a sample. Below is an example of a population that has been stratified.

This set of transactions contains negative numbers that represent customer credits. In addition to the actual dollar amount column there is and added column that uses the Excel absolute function "=abs(cell)" to transform all transactions into positive numbers. There are two strata in this example: all transactions less than or equal to $10 and all those over $10. The strata boundaries are determined by the absolute value of the transaction. All summary statistics such as mean and standard deviation for each stratum are determined by the actual dollar value of the transaction.

At this point we sort the transaction by the random number column but we use a two level sort. The first level is by strata and the second is by random number. If our goal is to have a random sample of five from each stratum then we can select the first five transactions from each:

ID	Amount	ABS Amount	Rand. Numb.	Strata
1	$1.00	$1.00	0.7486	1
2	$1.00	$1.00	0.1915	1
3	$1.29	$1.29	0.4426	1
4	($1.29)	$1.29	0.2578	1
5	$1.29	$1.29	0.3443	1
6	($2.00)	$2.00	0.6735	1
7	$5.00	$5.00	0.7964	1
8	$5.00	$5.00	0.0057	1
9	$5.00	$5.00	0.3452	1
10	($5.00)	$5.00	0.6381	1

11	$7.00	$7.00	0.1291	1
12	$9.00	$9.00	0.1892	1
13	$10.00	$10.00	0.5762	1
14	$24.95	$24.95	0.1299	2
15	$24.95	$24.95	0.8783	2
16	$24.95	$24.95	0.9081	2
17	$24.95	$24.95	0.0588	2
18	($27.99)	$27.99	0.5949	2
19	$27.99	$27.99	0.8048	2
20	$27.99	$27.99	0.9706	2
21	$27.99	$27.99	0.8529	2
22	$27.99	$27.99	0.4417	2
23	$39.99	$39.99	0.6941	2
24	($39.99)	$39.99	0.5731	2
25	$39.99	$39.99	0.3132	2

To calculate the true value of cost and revenue from a set of transactions, one would have to examine all of the transactions in that book. In practical terms, that is not feasible, especially when an audit population can contain hundreds of thousands or millions of transactions. If an auditor were to collect 1,000 or more random samples and calculate a projection for each and happens to know the true population value, that auditor would observe that half of the sample projections would be above the true population value and half would be below the true population value. Collectively, all the sample estimates would tend to converge onto the true book value in a pattern of the bell-shaped curve, also called the normal distribution. This is inherent in the mathematical behavior of random samples. If a random sample is properly drawn then its behavior is predictable within certain boundaries. Due to the bell shaped curve the auditor would also observe that some sample projections would be beyond the upper or lower 95% confidence limits. Those extreme values would be considered relatively rare i.e. occurring less than 5%.

Appendix V Getting Started

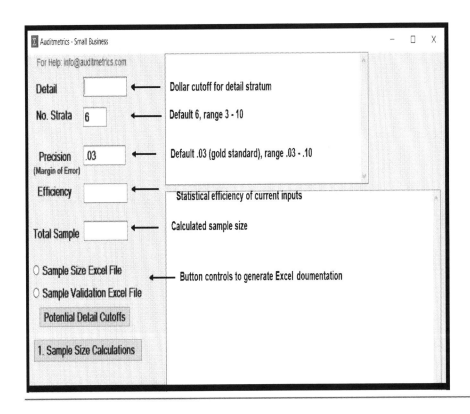

In this document is listed a step by step process of installing Auditmetrics and using test data to actually implement a statistical audit. Resources needed are:

MS Office Excel and Access

Windows NotePad text editor

Be sure to go through <u>ALL</u> of the steps. Failure to do so may leave out critical information.

Those statements that precede by a "!" are critical points to remember

1. Installing Auditmetrics

To install on a desktop download from Microsoft Store <u>OR</u> go to the install flash drive and click on the windows installer either SetupSB.msi or SetupPro.msi. Once installed an icon will be placed on the desktop. If you are on a company network it is best to contact IT.

2. Starting Auditmetrics

Click on the Auditmetrics icon and examine the main screen. You will see three data entry boxes: Detail, No. Strata and Precision. These are the basic inputs in designing a random sample for the statistical audit. Detail is the stratum of the largest dollar volume that is examined at 100% of the transactions. No. Strata is the total number of strata segments. Precision is equivalent to what the pollsters call margin of error. The default is 3% which is the gold standard for precision. In technical terms you are indicating that you want to be 95% confident that an estimate from a sample would be within 3% of the true book value. 95% confidence means that out of 100 random samples, 95 would be within 3% of the true book value. It is your mix of these three inputs that determine the required random sample size.

3. Test Data – Excel and Text File

There is included a test file, "Test_Population.xlsx". It is the book of transactions we will use to obtain a random sample. First, open the Excel file. The first row of the spreadsheet contains variable names. The column named amount is the transaction in which we are interested. Auditmetrics requires only four variables. Any other variables are relevant for a particular audit but not necessarily required by Auditmetrics. There is also a test Access file that we will discuss later.

Auditmetrics requires four variables, if not present, an error message will be displayed. They are indicated in red on the spreadsheet.

1. **Amount** – The transaction of interest in the analysis.

2. **Absamt** – Absolute value of each transaction. This variable **must** be sorted in ascending order. This is to handle credits.

3. **Transaction_ID** – an identifier for each transaction of the account, in this case it is a record count.

4. **DataSet** – A name to identify this dataset, valuable for internal controls e. g. date and other account info.

5. **Primary Key- Optional** – If a dataset is from a relational database with a primary key that links the various data tables, it is prudent to include this variable in the audit population to be sampled.

> **Variables 1 to 4 must be in the data file and spelled exactly as above. Any other variables are those relevant for the specific audit to be conducted.**

With the required variables above, letter case and order do not matter and absamt **must** be sorted in ascending order. If a dataset is from a relational database with a primary key that links various data tables it is prudent to include it in the total book to be sampled. In terms of statistics, total book is the "audit population" from which a sample is to be derived.

Transaction_ID has value when the data set is the merging of several data sources. For example, if you have two data sets of 1000 each and use MS Access to merge them into one file then Transaction_ID 1 to 1000 is from the first dataset and 1001 to 2000 from the second dataset. Transaction_ID also has value when filing with the IRS. For more details review *Appendix III – Random Sampling and IRS Directives* in the book.

4. Data Input – The Tab Delimited Text File

A spreadsheet is not useful for data processing unless you have specialized software for that purpose. Such software tends to be inefficient with several limitations that is explained in the book. However it is a simple matter to save the Excel file as a tab delimited text file which is universally accepted by a multitude of products including all major database and statistical software. It is just a simple matter of using "save as" in Excel and select "tab delimited text" for file output.

To look at the text file you should use a text editor. You can use your favorite text editor or Notepad that is available in all versions of Windows. If you are using the professional version of Auditmetrics and dealing with millions of records, it may be wise to invest in a more robust text editor such as IDM's Ultraedit®. It has a nice feature of making tabs in the tab delimited file visible.

! Transfer Excel test data to a Tab Delimited text file using "save as". Auditmetrics can handle all Excel currency formats including parenthesis for negative numbers. The only exception is negative numbers in red type only, which will not transfer as negative.

!When sharing data between several software products it is best to use in Excel General format for amount and absamt.

Auditmetrics has a powerful parser to handle input data. A problem may arise when sharing data with other software. Each may have its own quirks. The best policy, while in Excel, would be to always format amount and absamt as *General* rather than currency or accounting format. Auditmetrics can handle these formats but it is best to keep things simple.

5. Let's Get Started

Create on your computer a folder called Auditmetrics_Test and place the test data file. You can park your files of interest on any folder you wish to create. Click on the Auditmetrics icon to get started. Before calculating sample size you need three input values that are displayed on the screen:

Detail Cutoff

The first step is to determine high end statistical outliers, or in the terminology of stratified audit sampling, the "detail stratum." This is the stratum in which one does not rely on a sample but reviews 100% of all transactions. Eliminating the largest transactions from sampling results in a reduction of the variability (standard error) of the remaining transactions from which a sample will be drawn. This enhances statistical efficiency in that the detail stratum allows a direct review of all transaction with the greatest economic impact.

To start, click on the tab **"Potential Detail Cutoff"**. AI will provide a value for detail cutoff. A rule of thumb is that the detail stratum should represent approximately 1/3 of total dollar volume but Auditmetrics uses a more statistical analytical approach and for this data it is $7,500.

Also displayed are the upper percentile rankings of dollar volume. The auditor should initially spend time getting a sense of the distribution characteristics of the account to be audited. The auditor can vary detail cutoffs to determine if there is a more efficient input combination. The percentile rankings on the screen help in getting a sense of where the initial cutoff is located. As we cover the other inputs in determining proper sample size, you will find that you may get better results by tweaking all inputs.

! Professional Version, Auditmetrics-AI, has a button in the upper right hand corner that allows the "Potential Detail Cutoff" tab to also display Benford Law's first digit and second digit assessment. It is a useful forensic accounting tool to detect possible fraud.

You will also notice that what is also displayed is the interquartile range. This is the range of dollar amount that contains the middle 50% of the total audit population. Of the 25,152 transactions one half are between $14 and $205, 25% less than $14 and 25% above $205. This will give the auditor an additional detailed look of sample segments for possible errors or other potential problems. Each Segment may represent different products or services that require different benchmarks, staffing, marketing needs and monitoring methods in guiding performance.

When a file to be sampled is primarily dollar transactions it is a survey of the flow of dollars. What about customers or clients? When the basic unit is aggregated or detailed transactions then the analysis is an economic impact assessment. The auditor can look at different market segments based on the level of economic activity. If the file to be sampled contains other variables such as account id or a primary key from a relational database then the analysis can have access to other important variables such as zip code and customer demographics. The auditor can also segment the audit population into different market segments. Those segments can be geographic, demographic or level of economic activity.

Of course analysis depends on a validly drawn sample. Critical is how representative is the sample? Auditmetrics–AI statistical analytics guides you through the complex mathematics to assure such proper sampling. The goal is for you to have a sample that meets established statistical standards of the IRS, AICPA and the Multistate Tax Commission. Yes, anyone can draw a random sample but will it hold up under scrutiny? Will it provide tightly focused statistical estimates or estimates that act erratically? Only statistical analytics can assure an efficient sample and that is what AI does in the background which is transparent to the user.

The Number of Strata

Stratification is the process of dividing the population of transactions into segments (strata) based on a certain characteristic. In sampling based on dollars, one would stratify the population based on the dollar amount of the transaction. A stratified random sample will yield more precise results than an unrestricted random sample of the same size. Six strata is a default.

Precision

The default precision or margin of error on the screen is 3%. If the audit is for a formal submission to the IRS or state revenue agency, precision gold standard would be 3%. If you are conducting an internal audit and just want to get a preliminary look at the data then choose less precise values such as 5% or 7%. This will result in a smaller sample size.

Do a run with detail 7500 with precision and number of strata defaults. Then
Explore the interaction of detail, precision and number of strata impact on sample size.

D. Efficiency Factor

You should notice on the screen the measure "Efficiency Factor". The statistical issues surrounding this measure are better left to the book, but the higher the efficiency the better.

¡Once the three inputs are decided upon then select the "1. Sample Size Calculations" tab.

6. Generating the Sample

If the sample specifications displayed on the screen are acceptable, the next step is to generate the sample. Select tabs **"2. Select Random Sample"** and **"3. Sample Validation"** . That is all that is required and two random sample files will be generated: "SampleData.txt" and "SampleData.csv". The .csv file is a comma separated variable file which is a text file that can be directly read into Excel and saved as an Excel workbook. The .txt file uses a tab as a variable separator. Both files will be saved in the same folder that had originally been set up for the audit population data.

7. Documenting and Recording Results

Once you are satisfied with the sample as displayed on the screen, then spreadsheet templates should be generated that both help document and record audit results. As part of deciding on a final design, does the actual precision of the randomly selected sample actually match the original input precision used to determine sample size? Remember random means it is possible to have a sample with values that are outside of the original precision.

Statistical audits have an advantage over other types of sampling environments. The auditor selects samples from computerized accounting systems. Such systems can automatically summarize descriptions of the total book such as account totals and other measures. Therefore key audit population parameters are known. Suppose the precision in designing an audit sample is **set at 4%** of total dollar volume. A validity check would be to determine if a total dollar estimate derived from that sample does indeed fall within the 4% precision of the actual book total. Auditmetrics does this analysis and displays on the screen:

> **Observed sample precision under 0.04 no need to resample**
>
> **OR**
>
> **Observed sample precision over 0.04 need to resample**

If the precision test fails then re-run "**1. Sample Size Calculation**" to start the process again.
Redo steps 2 and 3 until the observed precision of the sample matches or is better than the precision used during sample design.

! This is an overall sample validation based on precision, the next validation test is a strata by strata statistical test.

The second validation test a pass/fail 95% confidence interval for each stratum. Its results will on the screen. If one or more strata fail then start again to calculate another sample and point and click until both validation test #1 and test #2 are passed.

! Only Proceed when all strata are designated "OK" and both tests are passed.

n	Mean	SD.	Total $		
69	22.74	22.78	1569	ok	ok
84	141.33	69.6	11871	ok	ok
89	418.15	174.03	37216	ok	ok
129	1001.66	404.51	129215	ok	ok
172	2108.62	955.52	362682	ok	ok
125	4412.92	2562.87	551614	ok	ok
451	30657.11	68197.67	13826355		

Validation #1- Observed precision under 0.03 no need to resample

Validation #2- Strata specific test passed.

8. Generating Excel Templates

After a specific sample design is decided upon, the next step is to document the sample with an Excel spreadsheet. You will now do one final run but this time it should be done with the following radio buttons selected.

The steps for documenting the sample:

• Sample Size Excel File
o Sample Validation Excel File

Select button **"1. Sample Size Calculation"** , **"2. Select Random Sample"**, and **"3. Sample Validation"**. The sample calculation step will run again but this time and generating an Excel file that will document sample specifics that should be shared with all interested parties.

The steps for sample validation and recording audit results:

o	Sample Size Excel File
•	Sample Validation Excel File

Then again select button **"1. Sample Size Calculation" "2. Select Random Sample"** and **"3. Sample Validation"**

! The spreadsheets are protected so that you cannot inadvertently write over a critical formula. If you need to make alterations then go to review at the top menu and select "unprotect sheet"

The spreadsheet exhibited below is a segment from the *sample section* from the validation spreadsheet. Each strata validity test has been passed. The column **"Amount Error"** is filled in by the auditor after totaling those transactions from the sample that are in error. The spreadsheet contains all of the Excel formulas to calculate the 95% confidence interval around the sample estimate of $33,500 of taxes owed. It should be noted that the 95% confidence interval displayed is a <u>one sided confidence interval</u> which is consistent with IRS directives.

Sample		Audit Results	Validity Check
Sample Total Value	Sample Size	Amount Error	
$1,011	41	$28	pass
$7,636	89	$225	pass
$14,486	94	$436	pass
$31,217	127	$916	pass
$58,512	138	$152	pass
$632,464	284	$6,325	
$112,861	489		
$745,325	773		
		Sample Error Rate =	0.025
		Overall Rate=	0.020
Detail Error	$6,325		
Sample Estimate:			
Lower Bound	$33,110		
Mid-Point	$33,500		
Upper Bound	$33,891		

9. Data Mining as a Sequel

Auditmetrics gets you started in sampling an account based on dollars. In business, dollars are the life blood of survival. With its templates, Auditmetrics can determine which dollars do not meet sufficient performance, in both absolute and percentage terms. You may have noticed that when a political poll is discussed in addition to the quantitative percentage result, most will discuss "what are the internals" of the poll. That means is how do the overall results relate to important breakdown factors such as gender, race, economic status and age. In statistics it is called crosstabs which exposes the underlying dynamics that help to plan future action. The original dollars is a quantitative variable while the factor breakdowns are called attributes.

What does this mean for small business? We are entering in a high tech commercial environment where huge commercial entities can marshal vast sophisticated programming to correct past deficiencies and search for potential opportunities. Auditmetrics helps the smaller enterprise to use accepted analytical tools that can fill in the void to survive in the modern economy.

Variable Sampling -Variable sampling involves quantitative measurable amounts and the result is rated on a continuous scale that measures the degree of conformity. Variable sampling is about checking "how much". For Auditmetrics we start with dollars as our variable.

Attribute Sampling- In attribute sampling the data result either conforms or does not conform. It is a method of measuring quality that consists of noting the presence or absence of some characteristic in each of the units under consideration.
Attribute sampling checks "how many Conform".

Excel functions ="frequency" and pivot tables are valuable tools in market analysis. Pivot table is a spreadsheet functionality that allows you to arrange and categorize attributes. It can be used to breakdown revenue by geographic categories, age breakdowns etc.

A histogram is a graphical representation (chart) of distribution data. A frequency distribution displays the number of data points that fall within specified ranges in a sample, for example dollar ranges. Dollar ranges are valuable for day-to-day marketing, histograms are commonly used in finance. Since finance affects every single business, understanding how to read, create, and manipulate data in the form of a histogram is critical for business owners and marketers.

Below is excerpted from a random sample that an auditor used to monitor the supply chain for a small manufacturing company:

Transactio	amount	absamt	PERIOD	Vendor	Strata	Error
22	421.43	421.43	3/1/2017	Jones & Sons	3	yes
24351	550	550	2/1/2016	ACE Dist.	3	no
8585	51	51	4/1/2015	ABC Co.	1	no
12345	7000	7000	3/1/2015	Smith Bros.	5	no
24376	10500	10500	6/1/2017	Acme Inc.	6	yes
14666	6034.48	6034.48	1/1/2015	Acme Inc.	5	no
80	9000	9000	2/1/2017	Smith Bros.	6	no
	.	.	.	.	.	.
	.	.	.	.	.	.

In conducting the audit a record was kept by the auditor to monitor which transactions contained errors. It was determined if a delivery was incomplete, faulty, delayed, the wrong supply or price etc. All costly delays in doing business. The Auditmetrics sample and templates documents the scope of the problem. But more is needed to guide the auditor towards a solution.

Using an Excel pivot table the auditor can now target corrective measures. A true attribute percentage would be how many transaction are in error. The percentage displayed below is based on how many dollars are in error providing a more detailed economic impact statement.

	Error By Vendor			Percent Error
Sum of amount	Error ▾			
Company ▾	no	yes	Grand Total	By Vendor
ABC Co.	$3,880,847	$166,861	$4,047,708	4%
ACE Dist.	$1,548,288	$159,263	$1,707,552	9%
Acme Inc.	$3,391,568	$398,518	$3,790,085	11%
Flower Inc.	$1,701,054	$205,547	$1,906,601	11%
Jones & Sons	$1,696,507	$405,821	$2,102,328	19%
Smith Bros.	$1,656,511	$112,436	$1,768,947	6%
Grand Total	$13,874,774	$1,448,446	$15,323,221	

In the text book, we discuss obtaining tab delimited data from Excel, MS Access, explained in Appendix II, and QuickBooks. For most businesses, these are the most common data transfer vehicles other than specialized tailored accounting systems. For large business the other potential data sources would probably require the input of an IT administrator or database manager. Despite the multitude of data inputs the output sample files are two, a tab delimited file and "comma separated variable" (CSV) text file. The CSV file has the advantage of being directly read in by Excel and can be immediately saved as an Excel workbook.

The sample data in this exercise was medical claims data contained in a single Excel spreadsheet. When dealing with large datasets or the need to merge several datasets, MS Office Access provides an easy way to do more complex data manipulations. If you are not familiar with Access then this is a good time to review Appendix II especially how to import/export tab delimited text files.

10. Data Trouble Shooting

The dataset for analysis requires a rectangular matrix with each variable a column and each individual transaction is a row. There are times when you think your data is all set for analysis and then you get the message:

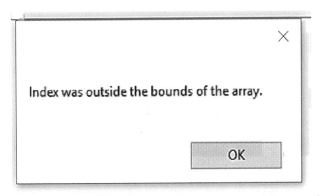

Index was outside the bounds of the array.

OK

This is a message thrown off by the operating system and the usual problem is there is something wrong with the data. Processing cannot continue. What generated this error message is that the original Excel file contained blank cells (row 15414) with no data or only partial data (row 15430):

Excel is a file manager not a database manager so when it is solely used as a data source, it may not be in the form of a rectangular data matrix with the columns as variables and rows containing individual data records. In this case the blank and partial rows are throwing off the Auditmetrics data parser. Sorting the file will help in determine if each row is complete.

	A	B	C	D	F
	DataSet	Transaction	Account	Name	Amount
15413	ERG	15410	107691	Acme Co.	15
15414					
15415	ERG	15412	310789	XYZ Co.	35
15428	ERG	15425	107691	Acme Co.	45
15429	ERG	15426	310789	XYZ Co.	12
15430	Workshop				
15431	ERG	15427	107691	Acme Co.	25
15432	ERG	15428	310789	XYZ Co.	32
15433	ERG	15429	310789	XYZ Co.	15

Solution Use Excel Data Sort:

Make sure that "my data" has headers" is indicated. Once you sort the spreadsheet you will notice the partial and bad lines either move to the bottom or top depending on the data and filter mechanism.

	A	B	C	D	F
	DataSet	Transaction	Account	Name	Amount
15413	ERG	15410	107691	Acme	15
15414	ERG	15412	310789	XYZ Co.	35
15415	ERG	15425	107691	Acme	45
15428	ERG	15426	310789	XYZ Co.	12
15429	ERG	15427	107691	Acme	25
15430	ERG	15428	310789	XYZ Co.	32
15431	ERG	15429	310789	XYZ Co.	15
15432					
15433	Workshop				

You can now eliminate the bad data and are left with a rectangular data matrix to generate a tab text file. This methodology is like the method used to derive data from QuickBooks standard reports described in the text.

Made in the USA
Monee, IL
18 June 2020